A HANDBOOK FOR HONORS PROGRAMS AT TWO-YEAR COLLEGES

by

Theresa A. James

Jeffrey A. Portnoy

Georgia Perimeter College

jportnoy@gpc.edu

General Editor, NCHC Monograph Series

National Collegiate Honors Council

Published in 2006 by
National Collegiate Honors Council
1100 Neihardt Residence Center
University of Nebraska-Lincoln
540 N. 16th Street
Lincoln, NE 68588-0627
(402) 472-9150
Fax: (402) 472-9152
Email: nchc@unlserve.unl.edu
http://www.NCHChonors.org

National Collegiate Honors Council

International Standard Book Number 0-9773623-5-3

Cover Design by Prof. P.J. Aievoli

Managing Editor: Mitch Pruitt
Production Editor: Cliff Jefferson
Wake Up Graphics, Birmingham, Alabama

Printed by: Commercial Printing Company, Birmingham, Alabama

CONTENTS

4

Theresa A. James

DEDICATION

When I received this project several years ago from the Two-Year Committee, I thought that I would just be editing a document finished by my predecessors. The copy I received has helped me to enhance the honors program here at South Florida Community College and has generally been full of ideas more mature and inventive than my own. It was not completed, however. Therefore, I accepted the challenge of finishing the manuscript.

This monograph is not intended to be all things to those in need. Some have wanted a monograph to establish the two-year college constituency of the National Collegiate Honors Council (NCHC). Others have wanted a monograph that defines exact and detailed guidelines for how honors in the two-year college should be done. What readers will get is an idea book for two-year institutions thinking of adding an honors program to their list of academic offerings. In this arena, it contains good ideas, and I think many people at two-year institutions (and perhaps others) will find a benefit from perusing these pages.

I have many, many people to thank. Herald Kane of the San Diego Community College District needs his moment in the sun for allowing me to volunteer to "finish editing this project," and I hope this small tome finds him healthy and wealthy (wisdom being quite out of bounds for both of us). I also thank Bill Senior of Broward Community College for allowing NCHC's Publications Board and me to use and to expand a bibliography he published in the National Honors Report *a few years ago. Thanks, Bill! I also wish to mention those who wrote the original pieces that went into this manuscript; full of ideas and drive, these people should have stars in their crowns. I was able to get several readers for the initial drafts of this work, and great thanks go to Eddie Weller and Norm Weiner for their diligent efforts. Special thanks to Jeff Portnoy. Thanks finally to the Two-Year Committee and the NCHC Publications Board for their trust and patience.*

Cheers!

Theresa A. James, Ph.D.
South Florida Community College
Avon Park, FL

Theresa A. James

INTRODUCTION

Only twenty-five or so years ago, as the 1980's began, the National Collegiate Honors Council (NCHC) Standing Committee on the Two-Year Colleges was dissolved for lack of participation from junior/community colleges. National surveys had shown that fewer than 10% of two-year institutions had honors programs and indicated no general agreement that they were even desirable. Much of the educational leadership in the country, including many in the community college hierarchy, relegated the two-year colleges to a permanent role of developmental, occupational, and continuing adult education.

That most socially sensitive and responsive component in higher education rebounded, however, with vigor and determination. Especially resilient and resourceful in the face of huge enrollment increases, budget shortfalls occasioned by difficult economic times and little political power, and a radical shift in student demographics, the two-year college found strength and inspiration in the very breadth of its comprehensive mission. Creative new programs appeared to balance the traditional, established programs.

The NCHC monograph *Honors in the Two-Year College* first appeared in 1983. By the mid 1980's, groups of community college representatives met, often outside the mainstream of academic times and places, and sometimes with interested colleagues from the university sector, to develop strategies for designing, funding, and managing honors curricula and full honors programs. The success of honors students after transfer to the university or in the workplace was becoming increasingly clear, not least to the students themselves.

Spurred by student and faculty enthusiasm for their classroom experience and aided by positive evaluations and a thirst for recognition and higher institutional profiles by administrations and elected governing boards, two-year honors programs burgeoned in the 1990's. Networking among institutions at regional and national conferences and the steadily increasing use of electronic communication pathways have spread information and support to these new programs. Consortia of honors-sensitive institutions have sprung up in many states (the Honors Transfer Council of California now numbers over forty colleges), and honors transfer agreements and alliances with four-year institutions are increasingly common.

The current institutional roster of NCHC reveals a two-year college institutional membership of 123 in a base of 773 institutional members; this total number includes the two-year programs. While these statistics do not indicate the additional professional memberships held by directors, deans, faculty, and students as individuals, they do indicate that the two-year institutional memberships constitute, at minimum, sixteen percent of the membership. Two-year colleges are fully represented on regional and national committees, and the landmark NCHC document "Basic Guidelines of a Fully Developed Honors Program" includes phraseology specifically inclusive of community college programs. One NCHC president, Ron Link of Miami-Dade College, in the 1990's was a community college honors director.

The trajectory of honors in the two-year program into a recognized position of leadership in American higher education continues as both its internal constituency and an increasing circle of supporters work together to increase access to affordable, high-quality education. In light of the rising level of excitement about honors programs at the two-year institution, the revitalized Two-Year College Committee of the NCHC is presenting this volume as an informational and descriptive guide for prospective programs and those contemplating changes or growth.

This volume is first and foremost an idea book, and as such aspires to provide a useful description of the many options available to honors education for the several audiences who, as a matter of course, may become stakeholders in the operation of a two-year college honors program:

- directors of beginning or developing programs, concerned with options for planning, implementing, managing, evaluating, and reporting;

- members of honors committees, seeking to bring wisdom and clear counsel to discussions of new possibilities and difficult issues;

- academic officers of a college, charged with overseeing a program and balancing its particular concerns with those of the total instructional program of an institution;

- senior administrators, college presidents, chancellors/superintendents, and appointed or publicly elected trustees, who develop and monitor the image of an institution in the broader community it serves;

- classroom faculty and their students, who may be enriched by a deeper understanding of their options;

- academic counselors and staff within and outside of a program, who weave the fabric of support services that engender student self-confidence and a commitment to succeed;

- four-year college honors directors, admissions officers, and student service officials, who may be seeking ways to mediate the transfer of honors students to their institutions, especially to their own honors programs;
- external evaluators, consultants, or regional accreditation representatives, who perform their functions periodically by institutional invitation or by state mandate for systematic college-wide program review.

Beyond their need for initial suggestions about starting a successful honors program at their home institutions, readers may consider the author's full and various descriptions as an invitation to lift their eyes toward the horizon, to envision a full program that will truly serve the needs of the institution. This work also acquaints the audience with a selection of key examples that will aid an embryonic program in the sometimes onerous birthing process.

Especially in the next chapter, "Designing an Honors Program," information abounds about alternative approaches to honors program design and management, even at very similar colleges. At the very least it helps readers appreciate the classic NCHC admonition: "No one model of an honors program can be superimposed on all … institutions" (NCHC "Characteristics" Appendix A). From the simple realization that one is not expected to consider descriptions as *prescriptions* can come the freedom and confidence to create a program that uniquely fits one's own institution, even if it fits no other.

The handbook closes with several appendices that list some useful research about honors, including a sample honors retreat and model honors contracts. The last appendix holds a bibliography of works in honors that combines a previously published bibliography by William A. Senior of Broward Community College with articles and monographs published by NCHC since Senior's work appeared.

CHAPTER ONE
DESIGNING AN HONORS PROGRAM

No set of rules for designing an Honors program exists. Each college must choose its own objectives, procedure, sequence, personnel, curriculum, and students. Among the many successful honors programs in two-year colleges, however, some similar components and stages exist. Those components in their many variations will be identified and discussed, and while the terms and vocabulary used here are familiar, each institution may decide on its own internal job titles, descriptions, and organization. The success in starting a program is more dependent upon the vision and commitment of the initiator(s) than upon the selection and sequence of steps.

The first stage is often the recognition of the need for an honors program. When an institution becomes interested in starting a program, one person or group of people will often lead the way, investigating options and benefits to the school and its students. What this may mean is that one of the first steps will be the selection of an honors director.

Because of its connection with the transfer function of the college and its emphasis on curricular excellence, an honors program must be at the very heart of the mission of the comprehensive community college. Because of this centrality of mission, the National Collegiate Honors Council (NCHC) recommends that the director of the honors program report to the chief academic officer of the college. If the program is to maintain a truly institution-wide focus, the person administratively responsible for the program needs to be in a position of sufficient authority and vision to help bring to realization the full promise of the honors program.

Since the program deals with students, faculty, and the instructional curriculum, the designers of the honors program may need to look to the faculty for their director. Indeed, directors may need to be faculty members of significant academic standing at the college. Such an academic has a high probability of having the needed experience to succeed as an honors director and maintain the respect of peers and the administration. In addition, a director will need to be as articulate, sensitive, and well organized as any manager at the college. The honors directors' external tasks will be wide and far ranging, for they will need to contact high school personnel, parents of students in high school, faculty and administrators of four-year colleges and universities, and community leaders who may be donors to the college's foundation.

Within the honors program, the director relates on a daily basis with honors faculty and students and can have a profound effect on the nature of the honors experience. Although directors may not have full control over personnel decisions, they will, in coordination with others, probably wield great influence over hiring by communicating the design of the program and clarifying its personnel needs. Therefore, they will need a good deal of savvy in dealing with diverse instructional departments and in negotiating with department chairs or division deans for the proper mix of honors courses and opportunities.

While support from senior administrators and the governing board of the institution is absolutely required, it is also essential that the faculty of the college and faculty leadership be intimately involved in the program. Since an honors program is intricately woven into instructional curricula, grassroots participation from the faculty is important. Taking the need for wide support into account, the honors director will almost immediately need an honors committee, usually made up of faculty, staff members, students, and administrators, and often intimately involved with the construction of the program. While different schools will need different skills from these leaders and will afford them different levels of authority, most will find that people of vision who are committed to education, to students, and to academic excellence and integrity, and who have superior management skills will serve best. The honors committee may be either advisory or policy making. If the committee is advisory, then its role is to offer recommendations, which the director can either accept or reject. If the committee is policy making, then it will be involved in setting the direction of the program.

The main concern for both director and committee, initially, will be to research other honors programs. Knowing the literature from such well-known national organizations as the NCHC and Phi Theta Kappa, the International Honors Society of the Two-Year College, and from the promotional and curricular material from other institutions, similar in size, mission, and complexity, the researchers will not need to invent an honors program from the ground up. NCHC and Phi Theta Kappa are especially eager to share ideas that have worked in the past and to send helpful material, including a list of trained consultants and evaluators. Researchers will also find that other schools have addressed the curricular and organizational issues they face. In addition to researching organizations and institutions, investigators will want to review articles published in educational journals relevant to honors programs, such as the *Journal of the National Collegiate Honors Council (JNCHC)*, the *National Honors Report (NHR)*, and *Honors in Practice (HIP)*.

Besides a review of the literature, sending the director and/or members of the honors committee to national and regional conferences is often a good investment. Attending the annual conference of NCHC or those held by the American Association of Community Colleges (AACC) or the National Institute for Staff and Organizational Development (NISOD) may prove useful. Wide coverage at these conventions will yield the greatest results; representatives may wish to attend those dealing directly with honors and with two-year colleges as well as those on more diverse topics, such as teaching innovations and best practices, technology and pedagogy, and student recruitment and retention.

The two year college might consider visiting honors programs at other schools or having someone from another program or a NCHC-recommended Site Visitor speak on the campus.

At some point, the director and the committee are going to have to write honors objectives and proposals. The program will be planned and described, including the philosophy, objectives, curriculum, target students, and program components. The program description will be most successful if it is invested in the mission of the college and fully integrated into the institution's self-evaluation strategy. Some criteria, for instance, may be needed for the selection and evaluation of faculty, syllabi, and support personnel. The program may call for the development of housing facilities, offices or buildings, personnel offices, student areas, and dedicated classrooms. The program description should provide details and justifications for budget requests, perhaps including resources for publications and publicity, conference travel, an office, and secretarial support. The plan may require a description of student recruitment, course scheduling, faculty training, and extracurricular activities and events. This program description will need to go through the normal channels for debate and approval required for any new program at the institution.

Once an honors program description has been accepted internally, relationships may be established externally, especially with other honors programs. Often, the best recruitment and retention tools are articulation agreements with four-year colleges.

As a final note on designing an honors program, no new program can be successful without a purpose that fits the mission of the institution. Even the most energetic honors personnel will hit institutional barriers unless the program is viewed as necessary and beneficial. Furthermore, the program should be designed to survive the inevitable changes in personnel that happen to every program.

CHAPTER TWO
ROLES IN THE HONORS PROGRAM

The Honors Director

The success of a well-planned honors program still depends on talented and dedicated people. The issue of personnel is equal in importance to that of institutionalization, or making the honors program an integral and necessary component of the college's mission. The people involved in the planning and subsequent administration of an honors program need to be flexible and have a genuine commitment if the program is to prosper.

The most important role in an honors program may appear under a number of different titles: honors coordinator, honors counselor, director of the honors major, director of the honors program, or chair of the honors council.

A detailed list of personal qualities beneficial to an honors director would, at minimum, start with high academic stature and standards—preferably a doctorate and tenure at the college—and the respect of colleagues and students. Those searching for someone to run an honors program will want to find someone who has talent in one or more of the following areas: teaching skills; administrative, managerial, and public relations skills; public speaking skills; and sales techniques. A successful honors director may have a visionary, flexible, and comprehensive perspective on honors education as well as a high energy level and the ability to motivate others. Since each director wears different hats at different times, and there is no successful honors director who has not had to do some on-the-job training, in the end, the optimal character traits are adaptability and patience.

The approach here is to introduce most of the possible functions that a director may be asked to undertake. The honors director usually has a committee, office assistance, and the regular administration of the college to help accomplish all of the necessary tasks. Therefore, each institution will decide what it wants its person in charge to do.

The official description of the position for the honors director should articulate specific duties. As the job expands with the program, the description of the position may have to be revised, and these moments are crucial in the negotiation and renegotiation of remuneration and benefits for the director. While the honors director will most likely be responsible in a number of different areas, the vague and all-encompassing lines of the position description should be kept to a minimum. How the institution evaluates employees, assesses programs, and incorporates institutional effectiveness must be considered. In establishing a program, the institution may need to reassign much of the director's time, as much as fifty to one-hundred percent, so that the director may accomplish the necessary tasks.

One of the first questions to be addressed and answered, after the position description, is where the functions of the honors program will be handled—in an honors office or in various administrative offices throughout the institution. For instance, will the honors program admit students, or will that be handled by the regular admissions office? Will the honors program advise and register students for classes, or will that be handled by the college's guidance personnel? This decision is left up to each institution; however, it is critical to understand how starting an honors program may increase the workload of some of the other departments.

However committees are formed at the institution, the honors director will play a large role in the management of the honors committee, including perhaps appointing the committee, managing communications and meetings, keeping minutes and records, carrying out policies, and updating official documentation such as the program description, procedures, or bylaws.

In fact, the management functions of the director cannot be overstated. In areas of student relations, budgeting, communications, report writing, presentations, and time management, the director's role is critical. Often, the director recruits new faculty into the program by helping them to develop an honors course. This type of course development requires the coordination of counseling, academic affairs, scheduling, course and faculty evaluation, and curriculum development.

Besides the crucial role of offering honors courses in the honors program, the behind-the-scenes role of holding meetings and keeping minutes/records and facilitating the flow of information to and from relevant offices around campus requires good organization. Such interaction may need to occur on many levels, including meetings with the honors committee, department or division heads, honors instructors, and honors students.

Honors directors may be the main source of information about the program at the institution, so they may need to be prepared with written or published information, or promotional materials: program brochures, course descriptions, program rules, policies, procedures, an operations handbook, and a student handbook. The director may be the first line of communication and may answer correspondence related to the program.

The program director may play a crucial role in recruiting students. Often, local area high schools and other feeders, such as home school organizations and non-traditional student organizations, will need to be contacted; high school counselors will need brochures and updates about changes in the program; prospective students may need the opportunity to ask the director questions directly. The director, most likely, may be the one to handle follow-up meetings, correspondence, and phoning. This type of networking is important for establishing a good relationship with the community and a good reputation with the local high schools. In addition, prospective students and high school counselors may be invited to campus for a visit, especially if the program has its own space or some distinctive viewable characteristics, such as a special study area, lab, or collection.

Directors may play an integral part during the student's application process—first, to get into the two-year honors program and, then, to transfer out of it. They may serve some of these functions alone or share the responsibilities with a committee, depending on the size of the program. The application dossiers of all candidates for admission to the program may have to be evaluated. Depending on the program, students may have to be notified of their status, so letters or calls or meetings may be necessary. If a student is not going to be accepted right away, there may be follow-up appointments or the creation of a document advising the student what additional tasks need to be accomplished along with deadlines; someone will have to monitor the conditionally accepted student's progress. If a student is automatically allowed to try honors courses, the honors director may monitor the student's progress, perhaps offering academic advice or other help, and then compare the student's progress to the program's graduation requirements.

After the director has successfully accepted students into the program, the students will probably need further advice and guidance in order to succeed. Most programs will have standards honors program students need to meet to remain in the program. For instance, they may have to maintain a minimum grade point average (GPA); in this case, the director, perhaps with the help of an academic advising staff member, will need to evaluate honors students' GPAs. Often, students will need to be reminded and warned about special considerations, such as minimum qualifications for transferring to a particular four-year college.

Given the prevalence of such programs as service learning and volunteerism in higher education today, students will also need to be provided with opportunities to show their leadership skills and involvement in or commitment to their community. They may wish to belong to professional or social organizations or may wish to have the honors program provide them with professional opportunities, such as internships or shadowing. Many programs will invite students to serve on standing committees; students will either have to be appointed to these positions or elected. Many students have experience creating and publishing newsletters, newspapers, or other publications like creative writing journals; if the program provides these opportunities, the director may be involved in some way. In order for students to be aware of all of the opportunities created for them, informational fliers, orientation sessions, luncheons, or other events may be useful. Finally, students may need to be acknowledged in some official way: a dinner, a ceremony, or a certificate. Such activities will also involve the participation of the honors director.

Besides managing the honors program locally, directors may need to interact with people and agencies outside of their own institution. In these interactions the directors will represent their college and its honors program. At home, directors may report on any work done or agreements produced from these contacts, direct all alliance programs with other honors programs or institutions, act as a liaison between the two institutions, and implement all policies and procedures necessary to uphold the contractual agreements between the two institutions. Such relationships with other institutions may come from affiliating with directors of other honors programs in the immediate area or, perhaps, from affiliating with and participating in the NCHC and regional and state honors organizations.

The director's participation in local, regional, and national conferences dealing with honors and related topics will probably take up a significant amount of time and, perhaps, money, especially when student participation at these conferences is promoted. For instance, the vast majority of directors have found it worthwhile to attend and participate in the NCHC Annual Conference and the annual meeting of the Two-Year Committee that takes place there. It is also useful to keep the NCHC and the home institution abreast of each other's policies, activities, and/or problems. All of the honors meetings, local, regional, and national, have proven to be excellent places for students, faculty, and directors to make presentations and share ideas about what works well. Getting involved in some of the lively discussions about issues related to honors can lead to improvement and progress in individual honors programs. In addition, an honors program may wish to emphasize undergraduate research or affiliate with scholarly and honorary organizations and societies, such as Phi Theta Kappa. Many of these societies have program requirements that will need to be learned, met, and monitored for compliance.

While paperwork can be time-consuming, there are rewarding and fulfilling tasks as well. One of the most pleasant tasks that an honors director has is to create and improve opportunities for students to receive financial support for their education. An alliance with the foundation or its equivalent at the home institution may result in a full scholarship program with a multi-faceted approach to dispersing funds dedicated solely to honors students and courses. In this case, additional scholarship funds may have to be procured from other parts of the college, agencies outside the institution, or donors. All of this fundraising is in addition to the director's normal institutional budgeting process. The director may have to attend fund-raisers or plan them as a separate honors occasion. If the director is successful in attracting financial support, scholarship rules will have to be written and approved, schedules for application and disbursement of funds established, and application forms and award letters written. Doing research to discover funding sources that have not yet been tapped and establishing relationships with scholarly organizations that offer student funding will also expand the funds available for scholarships. These efforts are often most appreciated by students in the honors program, and these funds will serve as powerful recruitment and retention tools.

The functions and tasks involved in an honors program call for office assistance, especially if the honors program has many students or many components. Some honors programs will require a secretary or assistant director. This person has to have more than standard secretarial skills of typing and organizing the office; he or she will need to assist in all of the functions for the director mentioned above and most likely interact with honors students on a daily basis and on a personal level. This person may serve as student advisor and counselor, activities coordinator, room scheduler, special events planner and host, photographer, and even chauffeur. Like the director, the effective assistant must be committed to the program and to the students. The optimal assistant needs to be an energetic person who can juggle many jobs at once—answering the phone, emailing, and collecting project money—and all this while planning ahead and getting the paperwork done for the major events throughout the year—ordering vans and reserving hotel rooms for student trips, preparing invitations and programs, and ordering refreshments. For those programs that do not have an assistant, the bulk of this responsibility may revert to the director or to other offices on campus that handle these tasks.

CHAPTER THREE
ROLES IN THE HONORS PROGRAM

Beyond the Honors Director

The honors director may occupy the most important role, especially when a program is new, but the institution must create an environment that will support the program when the honors director's mantle is passed to another person. To create such an environment, the honors program must be well established and accepted at all levels of the institution. Documentation of administrative decisions and other historical data should be carefully kept and should demonstrate how the honors program is intertwined with the essential elements of the college's mission. Here are some of the players who may represent ways of establishing an identity on campus and making the program indispensable.

Honors Committee

The honors committee may need people from many different areas, depending on the program. Students, members of the community, and other non-honors personnel may have creative ideas to offer a new honors program. The expertise of some or all of the following persons may be needed: the dean of students, a counselor, the student activities advisor, the admissions/records advisor, the articulation advisor, a foundation director, division or department chairs, a faculty senate representative, a union representative, and faculty representatives. A few words of caution: the more people included on this committee, the more difficult scheduling meetings will be. Even with frequent communications and virtual meetings, the group should convene in person at least once a semester or once a year. With a large group, some members of the committee may have competing values or interests. The best honors committee balances the commitment to excellence in honors education with a willingness to cooperate and experiment. Having a committee that will go along with anything the honors director says is often less productive than one might think because this committee may be charged with making sure standards are being met. A committee, however, that argues and labors its way through every decision will probably grind the director and the program to a nub. Too many strong personalities may impede the new program's ability to establish a footprint in the institution.

The honors committee may act as the steering committee to initiate and design an honors program. It may be formed later in the process and serve only in an advisory capacity or as a screening committee for applicants. It may be appointed by the college administration, the honors director, selected by the faculty senate, or composed of volunteers. The committee, at the very least, gives the program credibility and the director support.

The honors committee may need to meet on a regular basis, but this schedule will not rule out the occasional ad hoc meeting to deal with an issue or crisis. Some committees may meet less frequently because everyone is kept up-to-date by personal communication. If each member of the committee helps the honors program in a special area, such as scholarships, records, transfers, or discipline, then each person need not attend every meeting on every issue, provided everyone is receiving updates. The committee may need to meet more often if the institution has decided to keep the authority for the program in the hands of the committee rather than with the director.

While each institution is different, the honors committee may be involved in many of the following activities:

- determining and approving its own membership;

- establishing and updating program policies;

- ensuring compliance with program policies;

- selecting honors courses and determining curriculum;

- inviting, training, supervising, and evaluating honors instructors;

- conducting business related to the program;

- reviewing inter-institutional agreements with high schools, other two-year colleges, four-year colleges, and any other societies or agencies, and negotiating any needed changes;

- recommending sound inter-institutional agreements for approval;

- assisting in implementing the policies and procedures of the program;

- approving any exceptions to honors program requirements and/or approving all requests for honors independent studies (often called honors option agreements or honors contracts).

Faculty

Although an honors faculty needs to be varied and needs to reflect the make up of the faculty at the college, the honors faculty should be the outstanding classroom teachers at the college. Their methodology can vary. Although their philosophy and approach can vary to some extent, they need to love teaching, enjoy the students, and have the respect of their colleagues and students. They should exude enthusiasm for their discipline and inspire a curiosity on the part of the students. Most honors faculty members willingly attend honors events and write letters of recommendation for honors students.

Whatever the philosophical underpinning of the honors program, the honors director may wish to recruit faculty members whose methods agree with the philosophy of the program. These faculty members, in turn, may help the philosophy of the program to evolve as they discuss and debate teaching and learning. For instance, some faculty members make their classes as participatory as possible for the students; other faculty members may be gifted at presenting material through electronic explorations; still others may emphasize the idea that students must think for themselves. The honors program may call meetings on a regular basis so that everyone can share and describe their teaching styles, and the program can foster an ongoing conversation about teaching methodologies in the honors program. When instructors are brought on board, the honors director and committee may share the responsibility to train the new honors instructors and draw them into the discussion about teaching methodologies in the honors program. Honors instructors may wish to attend teaching conferences to provide background and material for debate. As the discussion progresses over time, the honors program will find that all instructional personnel are fully aware of the program's mission and responsible for updating it, as necessary.

Counselors/Advisors

Honors students need guidance and advice from counselors and advisors as much as do non-honors students, and perhaps more guidance because they have so many options available to them. Honors students have just as many pressures on them and difficulty making wise decisions as do non-honors students. Some honors students may even have special concerns and exit high school with preconceptions that may be counterproductive to their educational well-being. The personnel who come into contact with honors students as advisors or counselors, including the director, instructors, committee members, and academic advisors, need to have an understanding of the special situation of honors students. Honors students need guidance concerning their immediate curriculum, their long-range educational plans and scholarship opportunities, as well as advice concerning study habits, class loads, motivation, and attitude.

Many honors programs do their own advising. If the program is small, the director may provide this service. Given a large honors population, an honors program may need an assigned honors counselor and/or advisor. Where honors students rely on the regular counseling staff, two approaches are prevalent: in some cases, one counselor is designated the honors counselor in addition to the regular counseling duties. All honors students are then assigned to this counselor. The other approach is for all counselors to advise honors students. An initial orientation for the counseling staff and an annual review session are recommended if this approach is used.

Many academic advising departments today are using innovative methods to counsel and teach students, such as theme-based meetings or one credit hour classes to make sure that students are fully informed and are prepared for the challenges that college can pose. These approaches have proven beneficial both for residential programs, whose students may be away from home for the first time, and for commuter programs, whose students may not feel as much of a connection with the program or the same level of support from the program as residential students.

High School Recruiters

High school recruitment is essential for many successful honors programs. Sometimes the recruiting role can be filled by someone in the high school such as a counselor or one of the senior instructors. If feeder high schools have dual or joint enrollment, honors courses, a college prep or international baccalaureate program, one of the instructors may be trained to recruit for the honors program. The high school recruiter must be informed about the honors program at the two-year college and, more importantly, be convinced that it is a viable alternative to the first two years at a university. That person must have an appreciation of honors education. The honors director is often the most effective recruiter because of an understanding of, commitment to, and enthusiasm for the program. Honors students can make excellent recruiters at their alma maters if they are trained and supervised. They typically have credibility and often know students personally.

Depending on the service area for the college, representatives of the honors program may need to visit high schools and other locations. Once the honors program is up and working, videotapes or digital imaging of the various activities can be an effective recruiting tool if distributed to the area high school guidance offices. Honors literature—catalogs, brochures, a calendar of events, a schedule of classes, or *Peterson's Smart Choices: Honors Programs and Colleges*, the official guide to NCHC member institutions—can also be given to the high school guidance offices. Exceptional high school students may wish to go on honors field trips with the two-year institution or attend lectures and other high-profile events sponsored by the program. Such events can impress many potential new students as well as their parents.

CHAPTER FOUR
CORE OF THE PROGRAM

While the case has already been made in previous pages that the honors director has the most important role, it cannot be denied that an honors program needs some dynamic academic offerings. It needs classes that challenge the student in positive ways and prepare that student for even greater challenges at the four-year institution. Both the new honors program and established programs must make careful academic decisions.

The Curriculum

While the director, the honors committee, the institution or some combination of these elements will make decisions about what will comprise the core of the program, honors programs often contain a sequence or selection of courses and opportunities for leadership experiences and scholarly accomplishments.

Honors academic offerings vary from one institution to another, but here are some typical models:

- Honors sections of university parallel courses;
- Honors interdisciplinary courses;
- Team-taught or paired classes;
- Honors contracts in regular classes;
- Independent study classes;
- Internships;
- Honors Semesters at offsite locations.

Honors Sections

Special honors sections of university parallel courses are usually restricted to 10-20 students. The seminar-style instruction encourages student involvement. Although the course objectives are primarily the same as in the non-honors sections, the classes emphasize individual interpretation and analysis, creative thinking, oral communication, and writing. Often the texts differ from those in regular sections and emphasize use of original documents and recent journals. The level of discussion is usually more intellectual and probing, and the student outcomes for the course may emphasize an improvement of critical-thinking skills.

For example, some states have a common course numbering system. An honors section can be created for any one of those numbers should schools find it appropriate for their program. Freshman English or Freshman Composition is a common enough course, and a course description will most likely be on file with the state if it has common course numbering. An honors section of this course can keep this number and satisfy the Freshman English requirement if it fulfills the objectives of this shared course description. The methods used to accomplish these objectives are rarely prescribed. If a course must cover some of the modes of academic writing and the processes of producing a research paper, it can indeed perform these tasks in such a way as to create an exciting honors section that fulfills all requirements of Freshman English.

One important note must be added: each honors program will define what "honors" means, but there is considerable agreement among honors professionals that an honors section is not formed by adding more work to the regular course. The honors section of the course should embody the mission and objectives of the program, but that does not mean two extra novels in a literature course or an extra paper in a history course. When faculty members want to develop honors sections, the honors director takes responsibility to train them in the missions and objectives of the program. The National Collegiate Honors Council reinforces this definition of honors sections by including many panels on this subject at each annual convention.

Interdisciplinary Courses

Some honors programs offer an introductory interdisciplinary class. A few offer the entire honors curriculum through interdisciplinary classes. Many honors programs require an interdisciplinary class as a capstone class. As in other honors courses, the enrollment in interdisciplinary classes is usually held to 10-20 students.

An initial class often includes strategies for note-taking, studying, test taking, and research as well as a full discussion of the honors experience and honors student issues. The interdisciplinary nature of this type of class can come from choosing a reader that involves issues from different disciplines, from approaching one issue from a number of different directions, from exploring students' career ambitions and how different disciplines can lead to successful lives, or from inviting faculty from different disciplines to meet with the class on a rotating basis.

Honors programs that use an interdisciplinary approach throughout the curriculum may have a separate honors faculty. In this way, the honors director can negotiate issues of credit workload and overload without trampling upon any other department's planning and curriculum implementation. Finding a way to encourage non-honors faculty to cooperate with an interdisciplinary course, however, is often productive, and their involvement can add new ideas and approaches to the honors experience as well as carry honors practices back to the regular classroom.

The capstone class may focus on a particular issue or problem and approach it from the perspectives of various disciplines. Many of the capstone classes focus on the future, with a central goal being to prepare the students for the careers and academic challenges they will face. Many interdisciplinary classes use team teaching, guest lectures, field trips, and class projects. Often, students will produce a portfolio or final project that indicates their readiness to leave the two-year honors level.

Team-Taught or Paired Classes

A cross between the honors section and the interdisciplinary class is a pair of honor classes scheduled consecutively that students take as a unit. Classes in the same period of history, literature, or art may be taken as a pair. The professors can coordinate the study topics, outside field trips, guest speakers, and writing assignments. The professors may team-teach or coordinate their syllabi and assignments. While encouraging students to make connections across disciplines and classes, these pairs also promote community among the students in the honors program.

An example of this type of experience could entail scheduling speech and political science classes back to back. Students may be asked to write papers dealing with current political events in the political sciences course; the concentration in their speech class will be on speeches about current political issues. A third class, such as English composition, may be connected by a single theme or by emphasizing argumentative discourse, which would be featured in all of the classes. In any case, the instructors will cooperate to ensure that the students are making connections; they may find that attending the other instuctor's classes will help them to maintain the interdisciplinary nature of the courses. The students' final projects or portfolios may be presented in each of the classes or contain material from each of the classes. The possibilities for interconnecting courses will only be limited by the imagination and efforts of the faculty and administration involved.

Honors Contracts

An honors contract allows an honors student to earn honors credit in a non-honors class. Contract students should sign an agreement with their professors that they will complete a specified project. Usually the students are required to earn an A or B grade and submit an acceptable project to qualify for honors credit. The honors contract can be used to supplement the honors class offerings. In disciplines that do not offer honors sections—or when there are too few students for a class to make—the honors contract can accommodate the individual student who needs or desires honors credit. Usually the honors project must be submitted to and approved by the honors director and/or honors committee before honors credit is granted. Honors directors, in addition to the faculty member involved, should sign these formal contracts, and department chairs should either sign the contracts or receive a copy of the contract. Frequently, the projects are housed in the honors library for student use.

An alternative way to think about honors contracts exists at some institutions already: the honors lab. Many science and oral communications courses require a relevant lab. If there are too few students to justify the creation of a separate honors section of the course, students wishing to receive honors credit may be able to register for a separate lab. Often, instructor's remuneration for teaching labs is figured differently from their lecture section pay, and while some instructors will not be willing to teach another section of the lab, the honors program may find that department chairs and deans will not oppose the lab on economic grounds. Students in these courses will share the lecture with all of the students earning credit in that course, but the lab experience will be designed to follow the precepts and philosophy of the honors program at the institution.

Students may already be performing tasks that make them eligible for honors credit. Talented students may be so advanced in chemistry courses that they become assistants for the instructor. Perhaps they perform the labs before the regular students do just to see if the chemicals are working; they may maintain equipment or explain some of the concepts to the other students. If they had signed an honors contract before the class started, they would have earned honors credit. Caution should be taken that students are not just asked to read extra books or write an extra paper. Such assignments promote the unfortunate impression that honors courses are about more work, not a different experience. Any effort to trivialize the honors experience or make the classroom experience less than exciting and interactive will threaten the longevity or quality of the program. Furthermore, each honors program will have to decide what to do if the student signs the contract and does not fulfill the terms successfully, including whether or not the student has the option to cancel or void the contract entirely or must suffer clearly demarcated penalties.

Independent Study

Honors credit can also be earned through independent study. Some colleges reimburse the professor who supervises such an honors project. If such a project is permitted, it is usually not until the sophomore year. This project, like honors contracts, may need the approval of the honors director and/or the department chair or dean before honors credit is granted.

Many honors programs use this option, if they use it at all, to help students finish a final project or portfolio. If the honors program has a commitment to making the learning experience interactive and community based, then this option will probably not be appropriate for only one student at a time; a professor may have to take on several vocal, active, and participatory students to make this work qualify as an honors experience. If the honors program has a different emphasis, one that each student can complete individually, then an independent study would serve quite well.

Internships

Some honors programs provide experiential learning through service learning, a mentor program, or internships. Students are placed in offices under the mentorship of professionals in their chosen fields. In addition to their on-the-job training, they usually submit a written assignment relevant to the experience.

At the two-year level, students often find that they are not comfortable committing themselves entirely to one field or future profession. Honors directors often have to find professional experiences that help the students to grow in general terms rather than pursue a specific field. For instance, students may need leadership mentors; they could shadow, for example, the president of a local business for a period of time. Although students may never go into that business, they may learn many valuable lessons from that professional. Besides leadership, internships in communications, quality control, managerial skills, and volunteer work are not uncommon. Some mentoring experiences or internships are designed to help students narrow their preferences for a career path. This exciting opportunity is often what many honors students need to mature and develop adult ambitions. Service learning may be something that every honors course includes, depending on the honors program, but it may also provide the necessary components to create the honors experience for a few students or for students registered in regular classes.

While the people working in the honors program, the director and committee, the faculty, and the students, are really the heart and soul of an honors program, no academic program prospers without clearly defined and well-thought-out courses. Each institution will design a program's courses to fit not only its own students but its own institutional culture and history. With so many options for mixing and matching types of honors courses, each curriculum will have something special to offer.

CHAPTER FIVE
ADMISSIONS CRITERIA AND RECRUITMENT

Admissions Criteria

As is the case with many other aspects of an honors program, the kind of program, and its mission and goals, as well as local campus concerns, will determine the admissions criteria. If the honors program draws most of its population from the high schools in a particular service area, the honors director will probably have ready access to information about what tests those students generally take, what courses may be indicators of academic talent, what high school teachers are best able to identify honors-caliber students, and what programs have traditions that lead students to success in an honors environment. With such knowledge, directors may tailor admissions criteria to the area with little difficulty.

Because most honors programs draw students from a variety of sources, however, such specific admissions criteria geared to one or two high schools may not be complete. The typical admissions criteria often include scores on national tests, academic standing, GPA's, or transfer credits. A flexible attitude towards criteria will allow non-traditional students to enter the program and feel welcome, and specific criteria will enable directors to focus their recruiting effort and compile mailing lists.

The honors program will also have to decide whether to allow students who are not officially in the honors program to take honors classes. Different programs handle this issue differently, but tend to follow the simple funding logic based on enrollment in courses. That is, courses that make a certain enrollment time after time tend to be offered on a regular basis and lend stability to the program. Filling up the honors courses is, therefore, a priority and greatly appreciated by department chairs and deans. Non-honors enrollees may help with these numbers. Some programs make the non-honors enrollee obtain the instructor's or the director's permission. Alternatively, others allow students to enroll in honors courses if they have met with the honors counselor. Critical factors to consider when determining whether to include a non-honors student are the likelihood of the student being successful and the student's particular talents in that discipline. Some programs enroll students in the program and into classes based on the same criteria. In this case, all students in the class are going to have comparable skills, test-taking ability, or intelligence.

Given the basic similarities among honors programs in the United States, educators have identified three basic models of admissions criteria:

Uniform Standards

The following items are often used to set uniform standards for entrance into the program and the courses:

- Minimum cumulative GPA;

- SAT or ACT score—this criteria is usually expressed as a total number and as a minimum score on particular sections of the test. Programs often consider what the standard is in the area to define this criterion fairly;

- An essay offering proof of superior writing ability;

- Evidence of special competency or creativity, such as projects or a portfolio;

- Instructor recommendation(s);

- Signs of especially strong student motivation, perhaps determined through interviews, written proposals for academic work, or letters requesting special admission.

The easiest and quickest way to gain admittance to the honors program is to have appropriate test scores or GPA. Students desiring to enter the honors program based on alternative criteria may find that they must navigate extra steps in order to validate their participation, and that is why these criteria may be considered secondary or ancillary. The director, faculty, or honors committee may use these ancillary ways of admitting students who do not fit the primary criteria but who demonstrate great promise. The admissions criteria could be perceived as a barrier by some, but they can be expressed in a non-forbidding way.

The advantage of uniform standards is that they offer an objective basis from which occasional exceptions may be made. The objectivity of this basis provides consistent standards and, therefore, a degree of academic credibility. The disadvantage of this model is that it can be insensitive to underrepresented and non-traditional populations if the main criteria used are just GPA and test scores. The appearance of unfairness may be mitigated by phrasing admissions criteria carefully, by using alternative methods of entry, and by making a special effort to recruit underrepresented students.

Separate Standards

In this case, while admission to the honors program follows one set of standards, admission to individual classes follows a lower, provisional, or more flexible standard. The advantage of this model is that it is inclusive and encourages partial participation in the program for students who are partially qualified or potentially qualified for the honors program. Moreover, this model often can be useful to a new program to boost enrollment numbers and help new courses to be offered. The disadvantage of this model is that it requires elaborate tracking and updating of a student database to follow the progress of students as they become part of the regular honors program. Also, if exceptions become the rule, the program may suffer from the same disadvantage as the open-entry model, which is discussed below. The drawback is that a new program may tarnish its reputation in several possible ways: it could be associated with lower or arbitrary academic standards; students in the courses may not pass as often as they would like; and students who keep trying to get into the program may find it harder to graduate on time and may be disappointed not to graduate from the honors program.

Open Entry

Since many successful honors programs often attract students from all sections of the population, the honors program may need to be open to all interested students. Thus, the student who dropped out of high school, who came back to the community college, who is highly motivated, sometimes older, often a minority student, can be given a chance to excel in the two-year honors program, then become eligible to transfer to a university and compete with other students who went directly to the university. Since underrepresented or non-traditional students often do not fit neatly into uniform admissions criteria, an honors program will need to make provisions for attracting and nurturing these students.

In this light, some programs may choose admissions criteria that are non-selective. Students self-select into honors classes. Honors achievement is recognized when students meet exit criteria for completion of the program. It will be essential to make students aware of the nature and purpose of the program, so that they will choose honors courses and so that this decision has a high possibility of being a responsible choice for the student. Good communication will ensure that students understand the exit criteria before getting too far along in their course of study.

The advantage of this model is that it is in keeping with the open door ethic of many two-year colleges and is inclusive, not exclusive. The disadvantage of this model is that honors classes may sometimes lack the cohesion, sense of community, and intellectual rigor characteristic of the honors experience.

In actual practice, most programs have various combinations or permutations of the above models. The configuration of criteria of successful honors programs usually is flexible and sensitive to local campus concerns. A key dictum is that one should try what seems reasonable and then adjust the criteria as experience reveals the need for change. Inevitably, the criteria will need modification; no criteria should be thought of as absolute.

Entrance criteria and maintenance criteria for honors programs are sometimes different. The criteria to remain in good standing after entering a program may be slightly lower. For example, a program that may require a 3.25 GPA for entry may consider a student to be in good standing as long as the student's GPA is at least 3.00.

Then, too, entrance criteria and graduation criteria may differ in the other direction. A program may admit a student with 3.25 GPA but may expect the student to attain a 3.50 GPA before becoming eligible to graduate from the honors program. With recognition of different levels of achievement (3.50, 3.25, 3.00), it is possible for both lower maintenance criteria and higher graduation criteria to exist in the same honors program. The logic of the criteria should accommodate the students and the mission of the program.

Since some two-year college honors programs' curricular offerings consist mainly of honors-option contract opportunities, a word needs to be said about the participation criteria for these programs. An honors contract provides supplementary honors activities in conjunction with regular courses. In this case, the student who undertakes a contract may be required to meet the criteria for entry into the honors program. Within comprehensive honors programs, the criteria for undertaking these small-scale, directed-study projects may sometimes be higher than the minimum standard or maintenance criteria. The logic here is twofold: honors directors may need to conserve scarce resources, like faculty time and lab resources, and honors students will be more likely to succeed in an honors contract situation if they are the highest-caliber students.

Recruitment

Recruitment of students is always a paramount concern of any successful honors program. The most innovative and exciting curricula, the most dynamic and stimulating instructors, all come to naught without honors students to take advantage of them.

Reaching the Audience

The honors program at a two-year institution should begin with thoughtful and attractive offerings for the kind of students being recruited. Once the target audience of the program is clear, whether this is the top 10% of students whom the college traditionally serves or the top 5% of high school graduates whom the college has not recently attracted, the rule to follow is simple: **do anything to get the word out in a timely, accurate, and reliable manner. Then do it again and again and again**. Persistence is often what determines the difference between success and failure.

Recruitment Tools

Tangible Benefits

Since recruitment will consist of publicizing the honors program to the widest audience possible, the director should be clear on all the benefits of the program. Any discussions of such benefits will include a great variety of advantages. Some benefits such as special scholarships for honors students upon entry, during participation, or upon graduation are tangible; in fact, one program offers to all of its graduates scholarships of one kind or another at a four-year school upon graduation. Then, too, there may be other perks such as priority registration, extended library privileges, or library privileges at other institutions. Some programs guarantee admission to a four-year school. There may be the obvious distinctions of having "Honors Program Graduate" on one's transcript and on one's diploma. Another obvious advantage is having letters of recommendation written from the context of the honors program. Although these mundane advantages may not be the heart of any program, one should, nevertheless, be quite comfortable in enumerating them and should not underestimate their attractiveness to students.

Intangibles

The heart of the honors program will no doubt be in intangibles that provide high-quality education to able, high-achieving students. Whether that means providing a classical, humanities-based, interdisciplinary curriculum, a modern scientific and technological education at the frontiers of knowledge, or an honors post-modern vocational experience, remembering to communicate all of the advantages of the honors program is wise. These intangibles multiply as extracurricular experiences, community-building exercises, cultural enrichments, and academic enhancements are designed. Students who graduate from the honors program may be able to tell how they impressed an interviewer by discussing their leadership role in designing an honors program brochure or how their research for one class has evolved into a topic for a master's thesis. Therefore, having the mechanism in place to track students is essential. These successful experiences help future students and their parents and teachers understand how important honors education can be; an honors program can be marketed based on them. In the end, honors students realize that they have experienced an enhanced and fulfilling education that takes advantage of all of the cost savings of the two-year college experience.

Recruitment Targets

While any marketing effort should try to reach the largest audience possible, targeting the promotional efforts at specific audiences will make them more effective. The whole community of the college and its entire service areas will want to know about the special honors program offered at the local two-year institution, but many of them will not need to register for classes. An honors program has to reach out specifically to those parties interested in a high-quality college education. Several of the relevant groups of people are detailed below.

Reaching Students Already at the College

Many successful two-year programs are successful because they are inclusive. Recruiting students into the honors program from the current college population is a common way to increase enrollment and serve students. The following suggestions can be used in any combinations and can be adapted to fit any program:

- Data processing services can generate mailing labels and a list of all students with a GPA at or above the minimum standard of the program. These students may receive a letter, a brochure, or other important flyers containing information on the program, including honors program newsletters and descriptions of current or upcoming courses.

- Letters of invitation to join and certificates of accomplishment can be sent to students who make the dean's list or president's list each semester.

- At those institutions with a college-wide placement test, data processing should be able to generate mailing labels and a roster of all high scorers in a category, such as all those who qualify for freshman composition.

- Asking instructors and college counselors via flyer, memo, email, or in person to recommend students who may benefit from the honors experience typically generates a significant list of students to contact. Part-time instructors should, of course, be asked as well.

- Orientation meetings at the beginning of each term, at least one in the day and one in the evening, will provide access to the broadest audience of those interested in the program. Large or small, featuring a guest speaker or only the honors director, these meetings provide the opportunity for the even-slightly curious students to gather information and to expand their options for consideration.

- If the college has orientation sessions for all new students, the honors director should speak at these sessions. If these sessions are frequent or numerous, honors advisory committee members or properly trained and rehearsed honors students may speak on behalf of the honors program.

- Adult re-entry students or non-traditional students are capable and motivated students who belong in an honors program. They may be found in almost any area of the college including special programs for seniors, for women, or for disadvantaged students. For this reason, recruitment efforts should include the broadest audience possible. All who meet the participation criteria of the program and all those with potential who show an interest may be encouraged to try honors.

Creating a schedule of classes and catalog information that contain accurate and attractive information or display ads about the honors program is always a good idea. Flyers and other publicity about the honors program should be placed in strategic points on the campus: the cafeteria, the library, the counseling offices, and near registration lines.

If the sole target audience for recruitment consists of students already at the college, the program may be vulnerable to the objection that it is siphoning off the best and brightest students. In fact, many of the best and brightest students at the college will choose for their own reasons, such as lack of time, schedule conflicts, or fear of jeopardizing a high grade point average, not to participate in an honors program. So this concern is not one based upon the reality of the situation but rather on a misapprehension and a needless worry. Nevertheless, being aware of misapprehensions and addressing them as directly as possible would be prudent, for they can undermine the program if they are not quickly dispelled.

Reaching Students in High School

Indeed, if the high school recruitment activities are successful, the exact opposite of a brain drain will occur. Many academically able students who would not otherwise have come to the campus will matriculate. These students will not just take honors classes; they will take other classes at the two-year institution. Thus they will enrich the other classes at the college and enrich the general academic environment of the entire college.

So the other major group that may need recruitment is students entering directly from high school. Here, too, it is important to remember the recruitment mantra: **do anything to get the word out in a timely, accurate, and reliable manner. Then do it again and again and again**.

- Scholarships

    Offering scholarships to students who enter the program can be an attractive incentive to participate in the honors program. The two-year college foundation or its equivalent can be helpful in this regard. In one case, a donor wanted to award money to highly capable students at the local two-year college. Such a concern led to his funding scholarships for every student from area high schools with a GPA of 3.50 who attended that particular community college. Some programs are only able to offer reimbursement scholarships for success in honors classes or for lab fees. These awards are extremely helpful to high-achieving students and provide further motivation for them to succeed in their courses. In addition, these awards may provide unencumbered money if other scholarships have already paid tuition.

- High School Academic Challenges

    Academically challenging activities, such as a brain bowl or college bowl, provide a good opportunity for the honors program to be involved in the community. If these are a high-school-only activity, the two-year college students in the honors program can assist in producing the competitions and perhaps even in playing visible roles as coaches or mentors. If the activity involves other colleges, this is a fine opportunity for the honors program students to demonstrate their intellectual and academic acumen. In either case, the publicity is always useful.

- Dual/Joint Enrollment

  The honors program will have to decide if high school students enrolled in joint enrollment programs or dual enrollment courses will receive college honors credit as well as high school honors credit. Many successful honors programs recruit dual enrollment students into separate college honors courses. If this population is large enough, the honors program may wish to offer honors courses at the off-campus dual enrollment locations. Many programs allow the regular dual enrollment classes to be high school honors courses only and require that students who want college honors credit be registered in college honors courses. If this stipulation means that students must travel to the two-year college campus, programs can overcome the perception that the requirement is a hindrance to some students' participation by using it as another recruitment tool to entice students to campus. They may gain access to other services or special programs located on the campus.

- Summer Institutes

  Hosting a summer honors institute for high school students provides these students with an orientation to the honors program. If ninth through twelfth graders are on campus for other academic programs, they should participate in an orientation about the honors program and receive literature about it. If students have questions, keeping records of these inquiries and following up periodically, especially at key registration dates, will facilitate recruiting these prospective candidates.

- Direct Mail

  Many successful honors programs mail printed information to anyone who may be interested in the honors program. This strategy includes responding to all phone inquiries but also includes utilizing any other lists of prospective students. If the institution or honors program is part of an alliance with a four-year school, the names or mailing labels of all students from feeder high schools who are not taking advantage of an opportunity to matriculate there may be available. Also useful are lists of students at the high schools who are members of honorary societies, such as the National Honor Society and Quill and Scroll. If members of the faculty annually award prizes such as the Harvard Book Award to high school students or confer certificates from Phi Beta Kappa to high-achieving high school students, these names are useful additions to the program's mailing lists. Even if home addresses are not available, information can still be sent to these students in care of their high schools.

As is the case with mailings to students already on campus, mailing out not just the main promotional brochure but also supplementary materials such as descriptions of current courses, a current copy of the honors program newsletter, or details about upcoming events will underscore the advantages that honors offers.

- Director Involvement with High School Personnel

Advisors at the college who have regular contact with the high schools can be extremely valuable in spreading the word about honors. Having the honors director personally involved in this effort, however, is advantageous, for a myriad of questions about the honors program may be asked that only the honors director may have the insight or experience to answer.

One benefit of establishing a solid relationship with scholarship counselors at feeder high schools is that they can recommend bright students who, for financial or other reasons, might be considering the two-year college. Here is a perfect opportunity to transform necessity into a virtue. Once known, these likely recruits can be wooed with scholarship funds, literature about the program, an orientation visit or tea (or other special event), or put in contact with a student from that high school who is currently enjoying the honors program experience at the two-year college.

Finally, a supply of informational materials and applications should be sent to high school counselors and guidance directors on a timely annual schedule. Honors directors, members of the advisory committee, and honors students from particular high schools can be of service in delivering materials wherever they may be useful. Also helpful in recruitment are high school faculty members who graduated from two-year colleges.

- College Night

If feeder high schools sponsor a college night where representatives of other colleges and universities are present, the director or other program representative should be there to invite high school students to consider the high-quality, low-cost option available through the honors program at the two-year college. Discussing articulation agreements and alliance relationships with four-year schools may prove advantageous for promoting the two-year college honors experience as an option because of the close personal attention a student is likely to receive. Through the alliance with a four-year university, a student can still be assured of graduating from a prestigious university but without suffering through the large classes and impersonal treatment that freshmen and sophomores at large state universities often face. In addition, two years at the local community college often cost significantly less than those same two years at the four-year institution. While honors program directors may not wish to begin their promotions by mentioning the cost of higher education, certainly it may come up in the course of a presentation.

On occasions like this, the audience to whom the director is selling the honors program is as much the parents of students as the students themselves. Unless parents are exceedingly wealthy, the combination of high educational quality, personalized attention, and low cost will merit serious attention for the honors program. Even if some students do decide to go elsewhere, they may nonetheless spread the word about the program, which is a significant accomplishment. Moreover, the foundation has been laid for some reverse transfers by students who have been less than successful at the four-year schools or had some change of circumstance requiring their return home. Resurrecting the academic careers of students whose four-year experience was lacking is an important goal of many two-year honors programs.

- College Day and Speakers Bureau

In addition, scheduling a number of independent lectures or activities during a college day for honors students from feeder high schools is useful. These students should receive handouts in advance that establish a context and prepare them for the lectures or experiences on campus. Such occasions can be difficult to organize in metropolitan districts because they may require buses, hot dog lunches, and other amenities for perhaps thousands of students. Aside from the complex logistics of such an effort, some of the students may not be likely prospects. The effort, nevertheless, is helpful in generally broadcasting information about the honors program.

A prelude or follow-up to College Day is offering the services of faculty as guest speakers in high school honors and Advanced Placement (AP) classes. If sufficient interest exists, this effort itself may evolve into a speakers' bureau independent of College Day.

- Articulation Council and Articulation Projects

  Since the honors program will very naturally be involved in issues of articulation with four-year schools and with high schools, participating in institutional articulation efforts with feeder high schools is useful for the honors director.

  An honors presence in this arena can make key high school personnel aware of the substance of the honors program and even foster 2+2+2 programs hinging on honors academics. These initiatives use the last two years of high school, two years at the community college, and the last two years at the four-year institution to enable students to efficiently and economically progress to the baccalaureate degree.

- A Final Word

  Experimenting with and trying different strategies will reveal what works best in the local environment for developing and maintaining the program. Although not every attempt will be successful, much can be learned even from failures. What emerges as critical, however, is becoming comfortable with persistence.

CHAPTER SIX
PUBLICITY AND PUBLIC RELATIONS

Having defined some goals of the program, honors directors may wish to enlist the help and support of many of the faculty and administration as they prepare to recruit and enroll students. These allies will need appropriate materials and information to be conversant with the program. The program's accomplishments so far have been great, but the honors director has only just begun. If all effort stops after the program's goals and structure are identified, the honors program will remain a secret on campus. The honors director now needs to target information to the students who can benefit from the honors program. In other words, the honors program needs publicity.

Publicity takes many forms, serves many different needs, and must be tailored to the specific goals of each program. The honors director will need to think about how to proceed. The first impulse may be to take the ideas that have worked for other programs. That will only work, however, if the program being borrowed from is similar to the one being promoted for the first time. No two honors programs can be publicized or marketed in exactly the same way; nevertheless, some commonalities exist.

Honors publicity generally targets three groups: college employees, students, and the general public. The honors program needs to know why it must communicate with each group and how to measure success.

Target Groups

College Employees

• The Administration

Having gained the initial support of the administration, the honors director and the honors committee will want to keep administrators informed about what is happening in the program. Most honors programs are costly from the standpoint of cost per student hour; thus, the administration must understand how much the honors program adds to the mission of the institution.

• College's Governing Board

The two-year institution's governing board or board of trustees should be kept informed, especially about those elements that reflect the quality of the college. The governing board will likely provide an informal means of sharing information with members of the general population.

- The Faculty

  The honors director and committee will want the broadest base of support that can be had from the faculty, both those who are a part of the program and those who are not. The broader the support of the program from the faculty, the less likely it will be perceived as elitist.

- Foundation

  If the two-year college has a foundation or other collection of people with the responsibility of generating funds for the college, the honors director and committee will want them to know about the honors program. They will be able to use the academic successes of the honors program to solicit funds. The honors director and the honors committee, in turn, may be able to turn to them for scholarships and funds for special events or projects.

Alumni

Many alumni remain deeply interested in how their alma mater is doing academically. Certainly, as the honors program matures, the honors director and the honors committee will want to keep former honors students aware of the continuing activities of the program and achievements of the current students.

Students

- Desired Students

  This target group would seem to be the most obvious for publicity. This group is also the one that the honors director and honors committee will need to most clearly define so that all publicity efforts are successful. The goal of the honors program may be to attract more incoming freshmen or freshmen who are better prepared. The program may want to appeal to those students already on campus because many students may be ready for honors work after they have had at least one semester of college. One goal of publicizing the honors program may be to encourage students to stay to complete their first two years in the two-year institution's honors program before transferring to a four-year college. Contributing significantly to the graduation rate is one way the honors program repays the institution for its support.

- Students Participating in the Honors Program

  How the honors program communicates with the students who are already in the program will depend on the nature of the honors program and campus. If the honors program has honors sections, disseminating information through those classes will be fairly easy. Data processing services can often supply mailing labels for students in the program and for those students who meet the requirements but are not yet in the program. If the two-year college is a residential campus, then information can be given to the students through their mailboxes and posted flyers. The honors program will probably need an extensive email list of honors students. An easier way to keep honors students informed may be to create and update an online bulletin board. The work involved in keeping email lists and online postings updated may not be more than the work involved in keeping computer-generated lists updated. In all, the honors director and staff may find that managing the lists can quickly fill a significant amount of work time.

- Students Not Participating in the Program

  The great majority of students on campus will not participate in the honors program; however, these students can still benefit from having an honors program on their campus. It may make students feel better because the college they are attending has an honors program, which will enhance the reputation of the institution, and they may also benefit directly because honors events may be open to the whole student body. Fliers and handbills will be most useful for this population. They can also check the website or online bulletin board for events and calendars.

The General Public

- Specific Community Groups.

  These groups may have some impact on how the community views the college: service organizations, philanthropic groups, city and county governments, parents' associations, youth or religious groups. Many groups exist whose interest in one academic area could dovetail quite nicely with the honors program's ambitions. For instance, the honors program could offer a series of speakers on the history of the civil war and allow the local group of civil war buffs to help organize and publicize the speeches. These groups need to know what an excellent option honors at the two-year college can be.

- The General Population

  This group will be the hardest to connect with concerning the honors program because they are the most various. The honors director, however, may be particularly interested in them because they may underwrite the whole operation of the college through their tax support. Whether they pay salaries or define the two-year college's reputation in its service area, they will feel positive about the whole college if they know about the honors program's accomplishments.

Types of Publicity

After identifying the target groups, the honors director in conjunction with the honors committee must decide how the message is going to reach them. The following ideas need to be weighed and measured against the honors program, campus, and student body.

Before deciding on any type of publicity, the honors director should consider creating a phrase, logo, or brand to identify the honors program and all of the printed publicity that will be produced. This phrase or logo will immediately identify the honors program. In essence, this logo serves the same purpose as the mascot or team name used to identify a college's athletic teams. The people who produce designs for the institution should help the honors director produce the design and other material. The honors director also might want to see if students who are studying commercial art and design can participate in the creative process.

People at several levels of authority will want to be involved in choosing a promotional logo or phrase because these decisions will likely need to conform to the institution's long-term promotional plans. The honors program will not want to interfere with or undermine efforts by the larger institution to promote community awareness. The honors director and committee may have to have promotional items approved, and the honors program logo may have to coincide with or play off of the college's campus-wide logo. Establishing a link with the two-year college's community relations office may allow the honors director to avoid problems with publicity, promotions, communications, and recruitment further down the line.

Website

One of the most effective ways to publicize a program is to put it on the web. The honors director and committee may want to accomplish this goal in several ways: through campus/college pages maintained by professionals, through student-maintained pages that may or may not be linked to the two-year college's page, or through personal efforts.

Obviously, the director's ability to design and publish web pages will influence this decision. Having at least one page that does not have to be updated often and having some material that can be found by going to the college's web page would be wise. Beyond that, the amount and type of material published via the internet will have to do with the nature of the specific honors program. Electronically published material may be accessible for a long time, so maintenance will be required. The honors director may have to be careful about letting students open home pages in the name of the honors program, especially since the honors program may only have that student for two years.

Brochures

Most programs will want to have some kind of general explanatory brochure. This generic brochure may be altered to serve various populations. For a recruiting brochure for incoming students from the high schools, the honors director probably will want to have some kind of return card for them to mail back for ease of communication. Thus, this publication could begin with general information and save specific details for when the student makes contact. The honors program might want another general brochure for on-campus students, but without the mail-in reply form. Copies to community relations, enrollment management, recruiters, and board members will enhance the presence of the honors program on the two-year campus. Sometimes, students will want to become involved in the generation of these promotional materials, and this participation can often garner publicity for the program. Students in local high schools may be attracted to a program for which they, or people they know, can design publicity. Other brochures may not be purely informational; they may be concept brochures to show the character of the honors program without giving the details of admission, maintenance, and successful completion.

Posters

Posters would be a good opportunity to inform the general student body of the existence of the honors program. The major problem with posters, however, is that once they become familiar, people tend not to see them; in essence, the poster becomes just a part of the wall. Of course, the posters may be moved from one location to another so that the impact returns. As members of the public come on campus for various events, they will see the posters and learn about the honors program. The honors director might want to make sure that promotional posters are located in places where the general public is likely to pass while on campus. Local high schools may allow the honors program some of their bulletin board space to place posters, and monitoring the condition and placement of these posters, especially if they are not behind glass, will be especially important.

Bookmarks

One fairly simple way of getting at least one piece of information into the hands of students on campus is with a bookmark. The bookmark obviously contains a limited amount of information but would encourage interested students to contact the honors office. The bookmark might be placed at the checkout counter of the library for students. Or better yet, the campus bookstore could give one to students as they buy their books at the beginning of each semester. A bookmark should prominently and clearly depict one fact that would benefit students and entice them to keep the bookmark: a recent scholarship award, a quotation from a highly regarded publication, or the honors program director's official contact information. If the honors program maintains a website, this address will likely offer students everything they need in terms of information and updated calendars. For a new scholarship, a flurry of bookmarks may be the way to generate excitement.

Newsletter

If the two-year institution is not a resident campus or the honors program does not require all students to take the same classes, promotions about the honors program will have to be clever about communicating with all of the honors students. The honors office or director could mail memos out as the need arises, although such mailings can be costly and time consuming. The honors program may need some form of a newsletter published on a regular basis. Using a newsletter as a means of sharing information with students necessitates that it come out regularly.

The newsletter can, and should, contain information other than what might be included in memos to students. A look at upcoming events can be a helpful feature. Profiles of selected students can enhance the feeling of community within the honors program, especially if all of the students are not sharing some classes or living near each other. Publicizing events on campus is a way of demonstrating cooperation between the honors program and other parts of the campus. Short articles or pieces of writing by honors students and faculty can also generate interesting discussions and participation. Including a calendar with important events and deadlines is a good way to maintain student focus on success. A column may feature the activities and accomplishments of alumni of the program.

A newsletter has wide appeal. Alumni who want to know what is happening in the program can be placed on the mailing list. Certainly all of the teaching staff working directly with the program should receive the newsletter. Other staff, particularly the administration, should receive this information. While a newsletter can serve a number of purposes, drawbacks do exist. Newsletters are hard work to produce and must look professional, and from time-to-time, for example, the honors office or director may still need to send out a notice because an item missed the newsletter deadline.

Lists from Faculty and Follow-up

All instructors on campus should be asked to submit names of students who could benefit from being in the honors program. These requests can be made electronically and through flyers in faculty mailboxes. This idea could also be used with high school students through teachers who teach honors high school courses. The honors director may want to write a personal letter telling the student that he or she has been recommended by a teacher. The letter should include information about the program and an invitation to talk more with the honors advisor or to come to an academic program, social event, or honors class. Coordinating correspondence or contact with registration periods may mean that student interest translates into enrolling in honors courses. Sending a letter thanking faculty will ensure continued support for the honors program. Copying the department chair or dean would be a courteous as well as shrewd political move. Although letters may generate a response, in many cases a telephone call and the resulting personal contact and attention will be critical.

Presentations

Regular presentations at local high schools may improve the program's access to talented students and their teachers and parents. One way to interact with members of various community groups would be to make presentations at various meetings, such as those held by local community service or professional organizations or civic gatherings. The honors director can explain the program during these presentations, or selected students can make presentations about the work they are doing in the program. If demand warrants, the honors program might set up some form of a speakers' bureau.

Making reports or presentations to the two-year institution's governing board will enhance the honors program's reputation and visibility on the campus. The honors director may report to the board on a regular basis or save the presentations for special activities or awards.

Permanent Displays

Awards and other tangible evidence of the effectiveness and accomplishments of the honors program should be displayed in a prominent place. If the honors program has an honors office or some other identifiable honors space, this might be the appropriate place for a permanent display. Placing this cabinet or display where it can also be viewed by the passing general student body as well as honors students is desirable because it augments public awareness of the program.

Catalogs and Bulletins

The honors program should work with the college's registrar or other appropriate administrators to see that the honors program and its requirements are adequately displayed in the general college catalog as well as in each semester's course listing. Highlighting some special feature of the program in the course listing or bulletin reinforces the idea of the honors program in students' minds as they register. This is an excellent way for the general student population to have the honors program called to their attention as they are planning their course schedule. If possible, honors courses in the schedule of classes should be listed under the heading of honors as well as under the appropriate discipline.

Joint Sponsorship

When the honors program sponsors an event, organizers may want to have it sponsored in part by one or more other areas of the college. For example, if the honors program is bringing in a speaker for some honors program event, the student government, service learning program, related academic areas, or other offices in the college might jointly sponsor the individual. Through joint sponsorship, a variety of benefits can accrue: 1) maximizing funds by sharing the costs; 2) demonstrating that having an honors program on campus benefits all students; 3) having a larger audience interested in the event, thus more individuals attending and benefiting. Another ramification of asking others to co-sponsor events is that the honors program can expect to reinforce the connection by reciprocating in kind at a later event.

Press Releases

To let the general public know what is happening in the honors program, the college publicist and community relations office may need to be informed first so that they can use their connections and sources to publicize the honors program event. Local or weekly papers may print news articles about the honors program. Radio and television have to be considered within the overall picture created by the honors budget and the nature of the market. A talk-radio program may provide an alternative way to reach an audience, and many stations make public service announcements.

Counseling/Counselor

If the two-year college has academic advising done by full-time counselors, the honors program may want to have a handbook of information about the program for each counselor. In colleges where academic advising is done by faculty, the same procedure can work well. All parties involved should set a priority of referring students who have any interest in the honors program. This referral allows the honors program director to follow up with specific information for that student.

Honors Convocations and Awards Ceremonies

Recognition of the work and success of honors students is important in building pride in the honors program. This area is one where the nature of the local student body and the two-year college need to be taken into consideration. Although some honors programs have an exclusive honors ceremony, others host an all-college honors convocation where recognition is given to all students who have done outstanding academic work.

Public Service Projects

Some honors programs require that a student be involved in some form of community or public service as a part of the honors graduation requirements. Other programs use public service projects to bring together the students who are in the honors program so that they gain a sense of community. Whichever direction a program might choose to go, the results of what is done serve as excellent fodder for articles in various publications. This type of activity is also a positive way of letting members of the general public know about honors students and having honors students learn about the needs of the general public.

While publicity and public relations do not constitute the central focus of an academic program, the honors programs at two-year institutions certainly need to consider them. While an effective honors program depends on consistent enrollment and the retention of high-level students, the publicity from the honors program could well make or break its reputation with any number of stakeholders in the community. Therefore, even the loftiest academicians must spend resources on public relations.

CHAPTER SEVEN
ENRICHING THE PROGRAM

Once the honors program is in place, the honors director and the honors committee will continue to work on enhancements and expansions. The following suggestions are not listed in any particular order because the importance and success of each item will vary according to the needs of a particular honors program; however, honors directors should find some of the recommendations listed below helpful in the recruitment and retention of students and in the overall success of their program.

Assessment

One of the best ways to enhance the honors program is to become fully invested in the two-year institution's assessment process. Sometimes this process is called institutional effectiveness or quality management, but, whatever the title, it typically refers to the systematic self-evaluation of programs to see if stated goals have been achieved and to develop new goals within the context of the college's whole community. Some honors programs have been exempted from the reports, paperwork, or processes required of other programs.

When an honors program does not regularly assess and document its workings, one danger is that it risks becoming so deeply associated with one dynamic professor or administrator that they cannot survive the passing of honors program leadership from this person to any other person. When the honors program is well integrated into the processes and structures of the college, its chance of surviving the retirement of a charismatic leader is much improved.

A benefit of true integration for the honors program is that other programs on campus may find they have more in common with the honors program than they had previously thought; this connection would open up many opportunities for cooperation. Furthermore, these other programs that once may have characterized the honors program as elitist or unrealistic could find common ground for discussion and mutual benefit.

Generally, assessment involves the periodic evaluation of the honors program in a written report. The first step is usually self-assessment, writing up a list of goals and methods of achieving them that is published for the general college community. Often, these initial reports include a mission statement and a list of objectives that will be stored in a folder or database accessible through the college's computer systems. Considering the attributes of one's honors program in terms of NCHC's "Basic Characteristics" should be one of the first steps in the assessment process. (See Appendices A and B.) Should the college lack the resources to keep all of these reports on the computer system, the reports will still be available in one location, such as a dean's office or the library, since the assessment process is usually a community activity. Once a program states its initial purpose and goals, it will have to evaluate its progress toward those goals on a regular basis, possibly annually. These reports are often the place where the facts and statistics of the program's achievements can be collected and published for all interested parties to review. Many things can happen in these evaluations:

- the program manager may have decided to discard some goals, and this report will clearly explain if the goal has been rephrased, replaced, or simply eliminated;

- the program may have achieved a goal, and this achievement can be recorded; the report will then establish that this goal has been reached or that it will be reconstituted in the coming year;

- the program may have failed to achieve a goal, and the report will explain why it failed and how it will respond to that result, perhaps by trying again or discarding it as an inappropriate goal for the program.

Many interesting issues can emerge from these reports, especially if other programs on campus can be asked to indicate how they are contributing to honors education and adding to the value of the institution.

While this process may seem overwhelming and many associated with honors will claim that the benefits afforded by honors programs cannot be measured, full integration into the institutional assessment process is still worthwhile for any two-year institution thinking of starting or enhancing an honors program. This brief description should make the honors director and honors committee interested in this process, but all should be aware that the vocabulary used here often changes from institution to institution. Sometimes, the troublesome snarls in these processes can come about because of simple misunderstandings about words like "goals" and "objectives." (For an in-depth discussion of the nuts and bolts of assessment and evaluation, see the NCHC monograph by Rosalie Otero and Robert Spurrier.)

Retreats

Honors directors at two-year institutions take every opportunity to enhance the feeling of community among honors students, and an annual retreat has been used successfully at many institutions. For example, one college has a retreat near the beginning of the fall semester so that second-year students can welcome and become acquainted with first-year students. Besides familiarity with other honors students, the bonding experience can make new students more comfortable with the director. The retreat is usually organized around a theme; when it is the Phi Theta Kappa Study Topic, Phi Theta Kappa provides many useful supplemental materials. The current honors students prepare the materials before the retreat to produce activities and performances that help the new students to bond and to stretch their boundaries. Guest speakers, films, discussion groups, games, skits, a campfire, and other activities can work well at retreats. Secluding the retreaters at some camp or park away from all of the usual distractions is often a shrewd strategy. Usually, students have to be encouraged to attend, not because they do not want to go but because their lives are so busy; furthermore, many honors programs have strict rules about leaving schoolwork, cell phones, and other potential distractions back in civilization.

Honors Organizations

One of the ways to enrich an honors program is to participate in local, state, regional, and national honors organizations. Such groups can facilitate meeting other honors directors for the exchange of information or the development of academic alliances. They can also directly benefit honors students by providing opportunities to network, by offering scholarships and awards, or by sponsoring such activities as four-year college visitations.

If no local group exists, one could be started if the honors programs in the area cooperate and have good leadership. Honors programs need to consider membership in state, regional, and national organizations, particularly NCHC and Phi Theta Kappa International Honors Society for the Two-Year College.

NCHC is the most important national honors group for honors directors. NCHC publishes a monograph series, which includes this work, plus a newsletter delivered via email and available online. It also publishes a refereed journal dealing with the intricacies of honors programs called *Honors in Practice* (*HIP*), a refereed scholarly journal called the *Journal of the National Collegiate Honors Council* (*JNCHC*), and the *National Honors Report* (*NHR),* which is the organization's publication of official business. The organization's national convention has numerous sessions on all aspects of honors, including a growing number related specifically to honors in the two-year college. The Two-Year College Committee of NCHC also meets at the national convention held in the late fall to exchange information; honors directors, members of the honors faculty, honors students, and selected members of an honors committee will find a marketplace of ideas, brochures, and publications, and a vast network of cooperation. The conference program features workshops on Beginning in Honors© and Developing in Honors. In short, the NCHC convention is a great place to exchange ideas, focus the direction of the honors program, develop contacts with four-year colleges, foster relationships with local counterparts, and collect information on local, state, and regional honors meetings. NCHC has six autonomous regional affiliates that also meet annually. Attending a regional honors meeting will provide an excellent and relatively inexpensive place for students to present papers and meet with other honors students and for honors faculty and directors to meet colleagues and exchange ideas.

Phi Theta Kappa is an important national organization for honors students. With a history dating back to 1918 and with some 800 chapters, Phi Theta Kappa has had considerable experience with what works in honors at various levels of program development. By starting a Phi Theta Kappa chapter, the honors program will become part of an organization that prints numerous materials on how to enhance the success of the local chapter and the honors program in general; that publishes a newsletter and magazines; that offers millions of dollars in scholarships and other awards; that hosts a national convention attended by thousands of honors directors and students; and that sponsors an annual honors institute, honors topic, and service project. Obviously, the local Phi Theta Kappa chapter may help honors program recruitment.

Four-Year College Alliances

One positive outgrowth of honors programs is furthering articulation agreements among institutions because the vast majority of honors students are capable transfer students. The increased flow of highly successful transfer students between institutions continues to drive the articulation process.

Significantly, this flow is just a beginning and very naturally encourages a myriad of other articulation activities. As the honors program director sets up the channels to enable a successful transfer, an important collegial relationship is established with the university honors director because honors directors, regardless of their institutional affiliation, share the same general concerns about maintaining a high-quality education for able students. This kind of inter-institutional contact often leads to a transfer alliance between honors programs that will generate scholarship opportunities as well. NCHC has a Two-Year to Four-Year Articulation Committee charged with examining the issues involved with smooth transfers for students and long-term inter-program agreements.

One of the more tangible benefits of such an alliance for students may be some form of guaranteed admission to the four-year school. With such an alliance in place, other kinds of articulation become easier. Disciplinary faculty-to-faculty meetings can establish common understanding on what is taught at the community college and at the university. Articulation becomes truly collegial when the two-year and four-year colleges' faculties can meet to discuss transfer issues. As they negotiate different aspects of an articulation agreement, members of each faculty will be able to share and dispel some of their concerns and also to share some of their best ideas and have them disseminated. As a result of these faculty-to-faculty meetings, many courses at the two-year college are recognized as fulfilling requirements at the university. Therefore, all transfer students at the community college benefit from this faculty-to-faculty negotiation.

Students also benefit from this kind of relationship in more direct ways. One component of the relationship may be special orientations for students in the alliance, and these orientations can be tailored at the community college's request to the needs of the students transferring from the two-year honors program. Departmental counselors at the university can speak on departmental retention strategies and how students can be more successful. Students who have already transferred can talk about what affected their transfers, how rough or easy their transfers were, and what would have made a difference for them.

Such agreements may also include a guaranteed admission policy so honors students can enter their choice of majors upon transfer or receive special consideration for scholarships, campus parking, housing, or jobs. A transfer agreement can also lead to special counseling services, priority registration, library privileges, and free tickets to sporting and cultural events on the four-year college campus.

Beyond these student perquisites, creating four-year college alliances will generate other advantages; for example, such alliances can lead to meetings with other directors from two-year colleges that have developed similar alliances. These alliance meetings can become an important forum for the exchange of ideas. Alliances can also initiate faculty-to-faculty dialogues, better inter-institutional support services, and better communications with the counseling and admissions personnel at four-year colleges. In various ways, special alliances formed via the honors program will also bring the honors program closer to its feeder high schools since high school instruction and guidance personnel and students will be interested in knowing about these agreements with four-year institutions.

Of course, some people may resist the idea of an alliance, fearing that such agreements would reroute their potential freshmen to community colleges; however, most four-year colleges will not feel threatened. They will, in fact, like the idea that honors programs at two-year institutions are recruiting people for their institution, and they will see such alliances as guaranteeing that they will enroll the best transfer students: the graduates of the honors program. Initiating alliances with the four-year institutions to which honors students transfer may be a top priority for honors directors and honors committees.

To initiate an alliance, the honors director or the appropriate member of the honors committee should contact one or more of the following people at the colleges to which the honors program sends students: the admissions director, the articulation officer, the director of relations with schools or inter-institutional programs, the director of the honors program, or the college president or provost.

High School Alliances

Over and beyond a university articulation role, an honors program can encourage broader institutional articulation: 2+2+2 articulation—the last two years of high school, two years of community college, and two years at the baccalaureate-granting institution.

As was pointed out earlier, these articulation efforts take place because of the natural inter-institutional contact that an honors program engenders. Increased outreach to the feeder high schools produces better communication about the college to the high schools. Because of the impetus toward articulation, the directors of gifted and talented education at feeder high schools may be willing to serve on the honors program committee. When they do serve on this committee at the two-year college, they assure that the honors program is sensitive to the needs of its students. For example, if the high schools cannot offer an honors summer experience for lack of funding or lack of sophisticated scientific equipment, perhaps the community college can do so and can thereby encourage gifted, talented, and high-achieving high school students to consider the local two-year college seriously. Thus, the entire college benefits from this inter-institutional contact.

Developing a close relationship with feeder high schools will enhance recruitment and should eventually become an integral part of the honors program. The fact is, no matter how good the honors program, some of the more academically advanced students in high school will opt for going directly to a four-year college. While that choice is wise for many students, often it results from the pressure of peers, teachers, parents, and counselors who are unfamiliar with the benefits of attending a community college and of joining the local honors program. An honors director can help students fine-tune their decision by developing close ties to those groups that influence students and by spreading the word about honors at the two-year college.

Newsletters and Other Publications

A newsletter can be an important vehicle for staying in touch with students, faculty, alumni, and administration. The format of the newsletter will depend on the honors program's size and needs. Newsletters often include information on scholarships and transfer deadlines; program meeting dates and other calendar matters related to program activities; comments from the honors director, an administrator, a counselor, or perhaps the president of an honors society; a faculty profile; general program information; articles on how students can enhance their participation in the program; transfer information; and information on related organizations like Phi Theta Kappa. Newsletters can easily be enhanced with graphics and colored paper. Inventiveness and active honors student participation may make the newsletter one of the best elements of the honors program.

Once the newsletter is in place for a while, a journal or other publication may enrich the honors program. Such a publication, perhaps done only once a term or year, might include essays related to an honors topic or perhaps art or poetry, whatever proves to be most advantageous to the two-year institution. The important thing is that the honors program has created another vehicle through which bright students can express themselves and develop their potential.

Cultural, Social, and Educational Events

Having the students and faculty of the honors program participate together in social, cultural, and educational events can be an important means of creating close ties among the participants of the honors program and between the honors program and the community. Such activities can also become important fund-raising events and recruitment sessions.

Outings can include visits to a museum, perhaps utilizing the expertise of a local art instructor for the tour, or a potluck dinner hosted by one or more faculty members, or even a sporting or cultural event at one of the four-year colleges in the local area. (Complimentary tickets may be in order if the event is at a four-year institution to which the honors program sends quite a few transfer students.)

Events at the local two-year campus may provide cultural or social enhancement without the possible added investment of time and other resources involved in a long-distance field trip. In fact, the honors students can help to bring events to the local campus through fund-raising and other offers of sponsorship and help. A speakers program could be devised in conjunction with interested students, student government, or the debate club. The honors program could sponsor a scholastic competition and solicit contributions for scholarships as rewards from the two-year college's foundation, student government, or the college board. In short, the honors director can devise ways that students can get together to have fun, meet other students and faculty, develop their intellects, and maintain the visibility of the honors program. Such activities will likely generate goodwill among faculty towards the honors program and encourage honors students to become actively involved.

College and Community Service

For several reasons, many honors programs have a service component as part of their requirement for membership. One reason is that it instills in honors students a sense of social responsibility. Another is that many four-year institutions are not interested in giving scholarships to students who simply have a high GPA. Instead, they are looking for well-rounded individuals who have participated in school or community activities and who are willing to give something of themselves to their community and college. In addition, having honors students volunteer at the two-year college or in the community is another way to make the honors program visible and to distinguish honors students from other students. Requiring some sort of service will make honors students feel involved and enable members of the honors faculty, honors committee, or the honors director to write strong letters of recommendation.

Scholarships and Awards

To enhance the recruitment and retention aspects of the honors program, scholarships and awards to honors students should be as plentiful as the efforts of everyone associated with the honors program can make possible. The honors program can accomplish this goal, in part, by joining groups such as Phi Theta Kappa, which offers many scholarships and awards, or the honors program can raise money to offer its own awards. To do the latter, the honors program should have a representative approach various groups on campus for financial support, among them the student government, the college's foundation, and the local governing board. Also, local businesses may want to participate in enhancing their community by giving scholarship contributions. For specific expenses, the honors program may want to consider car washes, bake sales, and raffles, as well as other money-making activities the students can do. Fund-raising is another area in which students from the honors program may be able to cooperate with students from other programs or student organizations.

International Education

Participation in international education is yet another way to enhance the honors program. Students are excited by the prospect of international travel, and honors students are no exception. That the honors program may provide access to international study programs may appeal to students. The philosophy behind international education has many of the same goals as an honors program. Certainly, honors students will benefit from participating in an international education program, and affiliation with such a group will likely help the recruitment efforts of the honors program both in the high schools and on the two-year college campus.

Conclusion

The suggestions listed here are by no means exhaustive. Once the initial honors program is in place, the honors director might consider expanding the program to include one or more of the honors models discussed earlier in this monograph. The key is to remain flexible and take from different models those components that best suit the needs of the local population. Often, the best resources for developing the honors program further are close by: the honors committee, alumni, and, of course, current honors program students. These constituents may have helpful opinions about the different honors models as well as the evolution of the honors program. An honors mentality will no doubt enjoy the occasional inexpensive experiment, and while some of the experiments will not prove to be successful enhancements of the honors program, the purpose is to differentiate the honors program from the non-honors program, to enhance the honors students' experience, and to improve their chance of success in the future.

APPENDIX A

Basic Characteristics of a Fully Developed Honors Program

No one model of an honors program can be superimposed on all types of institutions. However, there are characteristics that are common to successful, fully developed honors programs. Listed below are those characteristics, although not all characteristics are necessary for an honors program to be considered a successful and/or fully developed honors program.

- A fully developed honors program should be carefully set up to accommodate the special needs and abilities of the undergraduate students it is designed to serve. This entails identifying the targeted student population by some clearly articulated set of criteria (e.g., GPA, SAT score, a written essay). A program with open admission needs to spell out expectations for retention in the program and for satisfactory completion of program requirements.

- The program should have a clear mandate from the institutional administration ideally in the form of a mission statement stating the objectives and responsibilities of the program and defining its place in both the administrative and academic structure of the institution. This mandate or mission statement should be such as to assure the permanence and stability of the program by guaranteeing an adequate budget and by avoiding any tendency to force the program to depend on temporary or spasmodic dedication of particular faculty members or administrators. In other words, the program should be fully institutionalized so as to build thereby a genuine tradition of excellence.

- The honors director should report to the chief academic officer of the institution.

- There should be an honors curriculum featuring special courses, seminars, colloquia, and independent study established in harmony with the mission statement and in response to the needs of the program.

- The program requirements themselves should include a substantial portion of the participants' undergraduate work, usually in the vicinity of 20% or 25% of their total course work and certainly no less than 15%. Students who successfully complete Honors Programs requirements should receive suitable institutional recognition. This can be accomplished by such measures as an appropriate notation on the student's academic transcript, separate listing of Honors Graduates in commencement programs, and the granting of an Honors degree.

- The program should be so formulated that it relates effectively both to all the college work for the degree (e.g., by satisfying general education requirements) and to the area of concentration, departmental specialization, or pre-professional or professional training.

- The program should be both visible and highly reputed throughout the institution so that it is perceived as providing standards and models of excellence for students and faculty across the campus.

- Faculty participating in the program should be fully identified with the aims of the program. They should be carefully selected on the basis of exceptional teaching skills and the ability to provide intellectual leadership to able students.

- The program should occupy suitable quarters constituting an honors center with such facilities as an honors library, lounge, reading rooms, personal computers, and other appropriate decor.

- The director or other administrative officer charged with administering the program should work in close collaboration with a committee or council of faculty members representing the colleges and/or departments served by the program.

- The program should have in place a committee of honors students to serve as liaison with the honors faculty committee or council who must keep the student group fully informed on the program and elicit their cooperation in evaluation and development. This student group should enjoy as much autonomy as possible conducting the business of the committee in representing the needs and concerns of all honors students to the administration, and it should also be included in governance, serving on the advisory/policy committee as well as constituting the group that governs the student association.

- There should be provisions for special academic counseling of honors students by uniquely qualified faculty and/or staff personnel.

- The honors program, in distinguishing itself from the rest of the institution, serves as a kind of laboratory within which faculty can try things they have always wanted to try but for which they could find no suitable outlet. When such efforts are demonstrated to be successful, they may well become institutionalized, thereby raising the general level of education within the college or university for all students. In this connection, the honors curriculum should serve as a prototype for educational practices that can work campus-wide in the future.

- The fully developed honors program must be open to continuous and critical review and be prepared to change in order to maintain its distinctive position of offering distinguished education to the best students in the institution.

- A fully developed program will emphasize the participatory nature of the honors educational process by adopting such measures as offering opportunities for students to participate in regional and national conferences, Honors Semesters, international programs, community service, and other forms of experiential education.

- Fully developed two-year and four-year honors programs will have articulation agreements by which honors graduates from two-year colleges are accepted into four-year honors programs when they meet previously agreed-upon requirements.

Approved by the NCHC Executive Committee March 1994

APPENDIX B

Basic Characteristics of a Fully Developed Honors College

An honors educational experience can occur in a wide variety of institutional settings. When institutions establish an honors college or embark upon a transition from an honors program to an honors college, they face a transformational moment. No one model defines this transformation. Although not all of the following characteristics are necessary to be considered a successful or fully developed honors college, the National Collegiate Honors Council recognizes these as representative:

- A fully developed honors college should incorporate the relevant characteristics of a fully developed honors program.

- A fully developed honors college should exist as an equal collegiate unit within a multi-collegiate university structure.

- The head of a fully developed honors college should be a dean reporting directly to the chief academic officer of the institution and serving as a full member of the Council of Deans, if one exists. The dean should be a full-time, 12-month appointment.

- The operational and staff budgets of fully developed honors colleges should provide resources at least comparable to other collegiate units of equivalent size.

- A fully developed honors college should exercise increased coordination and control of departmental honors where the college has emerged out of such a decentralized system.

- A fully developed honors college should exercise considerable control over honors recruitment and admissions, including the appropriate size of the incoming class. Admission to the honors college should be by separate application.

- An honors college should exercise considerable control over its policies, curriculum, and selection of faculty.

- The curriculum of a fully developed honors college should offer significant course opportunities across all four years of study.

- The curriculum of the fully developed honors college should constitute at least 20% of a student's degree program. An honors thesis or project should be required.

- Where the home university has a significant residential component, the fully developed honors college should offer substantial honors residential opportunities.

- The distinction awarded by a fully developed honors college should be announced at commencement, noted on the diploma, and featured on the student's final transcript.

- Like other colleges within the university, a fully developed honors college should be involved in alumni affairs and development and should have an external advisory board.

Approved by the NCHC Executive Committee June 2005

APPENDIX C

NCHC Publications, Monographs, and Resources

The National Office of the NCHC
1100 Neihardt Residence Center
University of Nebraska-Lincoln
540 N. 16th St.
Lincoln, NE 68588-0627

Phone: (402) 472-9150
Fax: (402) 472-9152
Email: nchc@unlserve.unl.edu
Website: www.nchchonors.org

Executive Director: Patti Speelman

View the NCHC website, "Available Materials," to investigate or order any of the following materials.

Of particular value to many readers is the full and objective overview of specific honors programs and colleges in America found in *Peterson's* guide. This official guide to the National Collegiate Honors Council includes both two-year and four-year honors programs and honors colleges; institutional profiles include a program description, participation requirements, instructions for admission, availability of scholarships, a description of the institution, and contact information.

Peterson's Smart Choices: Honors Programs & Colleges. 4th Edition. Edited by Joan Digby, 2005.

Periodicals:
Journal of the National Collegiate Honors Council (JNCHC)
A double-blind peer-reviewed journal for scholarly articles; two issues published annually.
Send inquiries to Ada Long, *JNCHC*, 316 Cook St., St George Island, FL 32328. Email: adalong@uab.edu; phone: (850) 927-3776.

Honors in Practice (HIP)
A double-blind peer-reviewed journal for articles describing practical suggestions and successful honors practices; one issue annually.
Send inquiries to Ada Long, *HIP*, 316 Cook St., St. George Island, FL 32328. Email: adalong@uab.edu; phone: (850) 927-3776.

National Honors Report (NHR)
The journal of record of the National Collegiate Honors Council; produced by the National Office and officers of the organization.
Send inquiries to nchc@unlserve.unl.edu.

Electronic Newsletter

Up-to-date news and information from the National Office of the NCHC.

Send inquiries to nchc@unlserve.unl.edu.

Listserv

Up-to-date news, information, and conversation; issues can be raised to the whole constituency of the NCHC who read the listserv; questions can be asked and answered.

Send inquiries to nchc@unlserve.unl.edu.

Monographs:

Each institution receives a copy of each monograph when it first joins NCHC and a copy of each new monograph as it is published.

Send inquiries about monograph topics to Jeffrey Portnoy, Georgia Perimeter College, Lawrenceville Campus, 1000 University Lane, Lawrenceville, GA 30043. Email: jportnoy@gpc.edu; phone: (678) 407-5324.

A Handbook for Honors Administrators. Ada Long, 1995.

Honors Programs at Smaller Colleges. 2nd Edition. Samuel Schuman, 1999.

Place as Text: Approaches to Active Learning. Edited by Bernice Braid and Ada Long, 2000.

Teaching and Learning in Honors. Edited by Cheryl L. Fuiks and Larry Clark, 2000.

Honors Composition: Historical Perspectives and Contemporary Practices. Annmarie Guzy, 2003.

Innovations in Undergraduate Research and Honors Education: Proceedings of the Second Schreyer National Conference. Edited by Josephine M. Carubia and Renata S. Engel, 2004.

Assessing and Evaluating Honors Programs and Honors Colleges: A Practical Handbook. Rosalie Otero and Robert Spurrier, 2005.

A Handbook for Honors Programs at Two-Year Colleges. Theresa James, 2006.

Beginning in Honors: A Handbook. 4th Edition. Samuel Schuman, 2006.

NCHC Handbook

This reservoir of information about NCHC and its membership is updated annually by the National Office and distributed to all members.

All the publications mentioned above may be purchased through the NCHC office or website.

APPENDIX D

Sample Honors Retreat

Building Community in a Commuter School: The Importance of a Fall Retreat

By Eddie Weller
San Jacinto College, South Campus

Without question one of the hardest problems confronting an honors program director at a community college or, for that matter any commuter school, is "how do we build a community spirit among our students?" With no on-campus dorms, students are not forced into contact with each other at all hours. With varied work schedules, students often arrive just before class and leave immediately following the end of lectures and labs. And with many external pulls, including family, work, and non-college friends, few undergraduates ever become close to a large group of students. For these and other reasons, many community college honors programs struggle to build camaraderie and esprit de corps among their participants.

San Jacinto College, South Campus, has had great success in breeching this wall through the use of a fall retreat. At the opening of school each August, the returning sophomores are boisterous and welcoming while most of the freshmen are often scared, hesitant, even quiet in our student honors lounge. This dichotomy continues until the retreat, which is generally held in the second or third week in September. After returning, the two groups have blended, and everyone is comfortable with each other. The building of the honors "community" has begun.

Of course retreats are not new to honors programs. I can remember attending TCU's honors retreat at Camp Carter in Fort Worth in the fall of my freshman year in 1979. While talking out on the small dock with a group of students until 4 A.M., I learned for the first time that I could converse about subjects that were larger than the small world I had lived in before college. That was part of the experience I wanted to pass on to each incoming class.

Since our first retreat in 1999, the program has grown and so has the retreat. Before our retreat students rarely came by the office and never stayed to talk with each other. After the retreat it became the meeting place for those who attended. And soon they brought others with them just to hang out in the lounge (a converted classroom). For over a year I had failed to get students to even drop by regularly. Since that first retreat, students are always in the lounge.

Included with this brief commentary is a generic model for a retreat that we have developed during the past few years and that works well for us. We do not try to reinvent the wheel every year; instead, we change the topic to keep the event fresh. Even so, there are several steps to success. First, the school must choose a topic that can challenge the students. We have found that the Phi Theta Kappa Study Topic is excellent. Each year Phi Theta Kappa looks at a topic in great detail. They develop a study guide (now available on the web at: http://www.ptk.org/) with many possible subtopics. The guide includes suggested reading materials, movies, and, importantly, thoughtful discussion questions.

Early each summer, I gather the returning students in the lounge in order to develop the program based on the Phi Theta Kappa topic. We spend time looking through the study guides I have printed off the Internet; ideally, some students have come by a few days early to pick them up so that they are familiar with them. We spend time narrowing the discussion questions until we find four or five questions, which we often tweak a bit, that we believe the students can address creatively in a skit. Next we look at the recommended movies and decide on one that will spark good discussion. For instance in 2002, with industrial causes of health problems the sub-topic under a more general topic of health care, we chose *Erin Brockovich*. In past years when the topic was water, we used the film *Dune*. Or when confronting the possible problems of the 21st Century, we chose *1984*.

After selecting the movie, we choose a keynote speaker from the faculty to kick off the retreat. The tone set by this speaker is incredibly important. Students usually know who is dynamic enough to wow the audience, but students also want hard information—facts and figures—from the speaker, outlining the problem. At the same time they want an expert and, of course, someone who is entertaining. While this prescription seems impossible to fill, we have succeeded each time. In each case the faculty member has been amazing. We pay a small honorarium to let them know how much we value what they are doing, but they more than earn it. In fact, in all but one year the faculty member has stayed for the entire retreat and even participated in the student skits.

After the intellectual portion of the planning is done, we decide on getting-to-know-you activities—from water balloon tosses to capture the flag—we start with a strenuous activity followed throughout the retreat by easier games and introductions. Traditionally, the sillier the getting-to-know-you games the better. These help offset the seriousness of the topics. Besides all students enjoy seeing their honors program director soaking wet from water balloons.

One of the highlights each year, after the speaker and the movie, is the campfire. Here the students are divided into groups to discuss the topic. Then, after often-heated conversations, they plan their skits. The faculty members normally stay until around midnight before hitting their bunks. Many of the students stay up all night; only a few will make it to bed before three or four in the morning. Because of the isolated nature of the camp we attend, there are no outside attractions to cause problems.

By the next day the students have become friends. They usually vie for the funniest skit, tell funny stories about late night events, and tease each other mercilessly. The director closes the retreat by tying together all of the skits, the film, and the speaker, and by making the campers laugh with funny awards for the students. As long as all the students receive an award, usually involving bad puns or events of the prior evening, they will feel part of the group and be happy—they have now been accepted.

Getting students to attend is the hardest part. We now require our scholarship recipients to attend, even if the college has to pay their way. With a guaranteed ten or fifteen, we then usually can attract around thirty students. And once students have attended one of these retreats as freshmen, they never fail to go again as sophomores. In fact, we have had several alums come back just for the retreat, where they tell stories of past retreats, building a lore that grows with our program.

Resources for Planning an Honors Program Retreat

Topics
Phi Theta Kappa home page
http://www.ptk.org/
Look at the Honors Topics links.
NCHC combines with Phi Theta Kappa to have satellite link-ups with member institutions for programs on the topic.

Camps
American Camping Association home page
http://www.acacamps.org/
ACA's Campfinder
http://search.acacamps.org/search.html

SJC's Top Ten Retreat Rules

1. No electronics allowed (CD players, gameboys, other individual games).

2. No playing cards allowed; only allow games that include large groups such as Trivial Pursuit, Outburst, Ubi.

3. No textbooks for studying.

4. No leaving and returning—everyone stays for the entire retreat.

5. No criticism allowed on the retreat—only positives.

6. No one left out because of cost—if a person can't afford it, college pays for it.

7. No bad attitudes allowed—everyone is equal and friendly.

8. All groups are assigned randomly—if cliques are already forming, disregard this rule and purposefully separate the clique members into separate groups.

9. Faculty should participate in activities, but should only act as catalysts in the discussions; faculty members should draw out quieter students.

10. If faculty members snore loudly, try to get them their own cabin.

San Jacinto College, South Campus
Generic Retreat Model

Day One

5:00 p.m.	Arrive - Go to cabins
5:30 - 6:00	Get-to-know-you game—high energy (examples)

- Water balloon toss
- Water balloon/water gun fight
- Volleyball
- Capture the flag

6:00 - 6:30	Dinner
6:45 - 7:00	Get-to-know-you game—low energy (examples)

- Identify the famous person whose name is on your back
- Grid with descriptions on it—find someone who fits the description
- Break into groups of three and interview each other, then rotate the groups

7:00 - 7:30	Keynote speaker: introduces theme of the retreat—faculty member
7:30 - 7:45	Break—always have plenty of soft drinks, water, and snacks!
7:45 - 9:45	Thematic movie
10:00	Campfire

Break into random discussion groups

- Groups done randomly by dots on the name tags or other method
- Discussion questions taken/modified from Phi Theta Kappa suggestions
- Make certain questions are controversial to start a discussion
- After some discussion, begin trying to think of a way to visually portray the discussion through a skit, etc.

Smores

12:00 (Midnight)	Faculty to bed
	Deep discussions usually continue
	Free time

Day Two

8:30 a.m.	Breakfast
9:00 - 10:00	Finalize skits to explain the discussion question
10:30 - 11:00	Skits
11:00 - 11:30	Closing remarks—tie it all together—by the director or a faculty member
	Add a humorous side:

- Silly awards to the students
- Limericks

11:30	Pack it up
12:00 (noon)	Lunch and leave

APPENDIX E

Sample Contracts between Students and Programs for Honors Credit

These samples were excerpted, literally ripped, from a collection prepared by Roy Colquitt, *A "Sampler" of Honors Contracts.* I have excerpted samples from two-year institutions concerning both courses for transfer and non-transfer credit. The documents have not been updated, but they have been slightly altered and formatted for this publication.

Here is a listing in order. Some of the multi-page or double-sided documents read on subsequent pages.

1. Broward Community College (2 pages)

2. Johnson County Community College (7 pages)

3. Northeast Community College (4 pages)

4. Oklahoma City Community College (1 page)

5. Palm Beach Community College (5 pages)

6. Reading Area Community College (4 pages)

7. Redlands Community College (1 page)

HONORS BY CONTRACT
Broward Community College
Honors & Scholars Programs   ***Please Print or Type.***

APPLICATION

Term: _____
Campus: _____

Student Name (Last, First, Middle): _____

Student I.D. No.: _____

Course Title: _____

Sequence No.: _____   Course Prefix: _____

Course No.: _____   Section No.: _____

Professor: _____   Dept: _____

DIRECTIONS

1. By the end of the fourth week of classes, the student must submit the "Honors by Contract" to the professor and then immediately to the Honors Director/Coordinator for approval.

2. The "Honors by Contract" must be accompanied by a typed 250-word proposal describing the Honors project.

3. Where appropriate the proposal should have a working bibliography. In the case of math or science projects, the primary text(s) should be cited.

4. After all signatures have been acquired, the student, professor, and Honors Director/Coordinator will each keep a copy of the "Honors by Contract" and the 250-word proposal.

5. The Grade Certification of the "Honors by Contract," together with a copy of the Honors project, must be turned in to the Honors Director/Coordinator by the Final Exam date.

_____   _____
Student   Date   Authorized Approval Signature (Professor)   Date
I request/agree to do the above project
to earn Honors Credit for this course.   Director/Coordinator, Honors & Scholars Program   Date

GRADE CERTIFICATION

HONORS PROJECT COMPLETED AND ACCEPTABLE: YES: ____ NO: ____
Note: A Grade of an "A" must be earned for "Honors by Contract" Credit.

GRADE EARNED ON PAPER: _____   GRADE EARNED FOR CLASS: _____

I certify the above-named student has satisfactorily completed the Honors Course Project according to the standards of the Honors and Scholars Program.

_____   _____
Date Signed   Professor

_____   _____
Date Signed   Director/Coordinator, Honors Scholars Program

*Please write "HONORS" next to the Grade of "A" in the Class Grade Report.

HONORS BY CONTRACT INSTRUCTIONS

ELIGIBILITY FOR PARTICIPATION

Students must be members of the Honors Institute and have completed honors classes.

Preferably, professors will be full-time members of the faculty.

PROJECT GUIDELINES & PROCEDURES

1. An "Honors by Contract" form should be obtained from the Honors Coordinator and filled out by the end of the fourth week of the semester. This form is then returned to the Honors Coordinator, who signs it. After all signatures have been obtained, the Professor keeps the original, and the student and Honors Coordinator keep copies.

2. A typed 250-word proposal of the research project, together with a working bibliography, must be submitted at the time of application.

3. A typical honors project consists of the following: a typed 3,000-word research paper that is original in style and content and represents a comprehensive study of a topic pertinent to the course. Specific departmental guidelines have been prepared for math and science honors projects.

4. The "Honors by Contract" project paper must be submitted **in addition** to any writing requirements that the course may originally carry.

5. In order for a student to be given credit for an "Honors by Contract" course, he or she must earn an "A" in the class and on the project.

6. At the completion of the project, the professor will grade it, sign the Grade Certification section of the "Honors by Contract," and return both the "Honors by Contract" and the paper (project) to the Campus Honors Coordinator for forwarding to the Honors Institute College-wide Office for final approval by the Director.

7. After approval by the Director, a memorandum is sent to the Registrar, Fort Lauderdale Center, to have Honors Credit entered on the student's record.

NURS 121/122   Revised Spring 20XX

JOHNSON COUNTY COMMUNITY COLLEGE
HONORS PROGRAM

Johnson County Community College provides a range of services to allow persons with disabilities to participate in educational programs and activities. If you desire support services, contact the Student Access Center (913) 4XX-XXXX, Ext. 3XXX, or TDD 4XX-XXXX.

DESCRIPTION OF HONORS CONTRACT

This Honors Contract MUST be taken concurrently with the following course:

Course Title: Concepts of Health, NURS 121/122

(course allowing the contract)

Mentor: C——— D——

Hours Credit: 1

Student's Name: _____

In addition to satisfying the normal objectives/competencies of the course, the student must complete the following additional objectives to accomplish a higher level of scholastic work:

Objectives:

1. Describe both verbally and in writing a comprehensive exploration of a topic (or project) relevant to current or future nursing practice.

2. Demonstrate acquired literature and library search skills.

3. Evaluate current nursing research and scholarly publications.

4. Identify available community resources (e.g., American Heart Association, Midwest Organ Bank, Clinical Nurse Specialists) that could be used to enhance patient care.

5. Recognize nursing issues/topics/problems needing future exploration or research.

Tasks:

1. A computer search at JCCC, assisted by library staff.

2. Research on topic selected using journals available at JCCC and/or articles obtained via inter-library facilities.

3. A visit to at least one community resource agency.

4. A formally written research paper on the topic selected or the completion of a nursing-related project.

NURS 121/122

5. The research paper will include the following:

    a. Introduction of topic, including background about why the topic is relevant to nursing today.

    b. Current research, trends, and theories.

    c. Information regarding the usefulness of the visit to the nursing resource facility.

    d. Conclusions.

    e. Recommendations for future research/projects.

    f. Properly formatted references.

    g. Presentation of findings to mentor and/or peer group.

6. The project will include the following:

    a. A brief, but formally written paper describing the selected project and containing these elements:

        1. A statement explaining why the project was selected and how the project relates to current nursing practice.

        2. Current research, trends, and theories that relate to the development of the selected project.

        3. A listing of nursing resources used during the development of the project.

        4. Your plans for using the project.

        5. A summary of the benefits you derived from completing the project.

        6. Properly formatted references.

    b. A copy of the completed project (health questionnaire, video-tape tutorial, teaching project, etc.).

    c. A service-learning component to the project may be completed using guidelines set up by the Service Learning Department. This will include visits to a service-learning site as well as actual service rendered at the site.

NURS 121/122

Conferences:

Week	Material Covered/Process
1 & 2	Review and sign contract
3	Select topic, meet with mentor.
	* Select service-learning experience.
4	Background reading on topic. Discussion of topic selection with mentor.
5	Computer search (at JCCC). Meet with mentor to discuss interpretation of printout and obtaining specific journal articles. Obtain handout from Writing Center (at JCCC) on writing papers. Begin independent research or planning for project.
	* Have an interview with M———— S———— and receive a service-learning placement.
6-8	Meet with mentor to discuss possible visits or interviews and set dates for same. Have written outline prepared or project parameters defined.
	* Visit service-learning site and begin service experience. Submit reflection journal related to service-learning experience.
9-10	Meet with mentor to discuss progress.
	* Discuss service-learning experience with mentor.
11	Report to mentor about site visits or interviews and the progress of written paper or project development.
12-14	Independent work. Meet at least once with mentor to discuss progress.
	* Continue service-learning participation at site and turn in reflection journal about experience. Discuss experience with mentor.
15	Presentation of paper or project to mentor and/or peer group, if desired.
	* Ten hours of service must be completed.
16	Make any recommended corrections. Turn in final paper.
	* Service-Learning Outcomes Assessment is due.

* To be completed if Service-Learning Project is selected.

Expectations:

1. To acquire the tools necessary for independent learning in the area of nursing and familiarize the student with available nursing literature.

2. To stimulate critical thinking and give the student an opportunity to pursue a challenging project in the area of nursing.

3. To demonstrate to the student the numerous possibilities for study and research in the area of nursing.

4. To familiarize the student with nursing resources available in the greater Kansas City area.

5. To experience learning through an optional service-learning component in which the student volunteers at an approved community-agency site.

Grading Criteria:

The grade will be determined as follows: 60% based on the quality of the paper and/or project and 40% on the student's ability to discuss the selected topic in depth. If the service-learning component is chosen, it will comprise 30% of the course grade: 20% from the quality of experiential learning presented in a paper and/or project and 10% by the student's ability to discuss the experience in depth.

JOHNSON COUNTY COMMUNITY COLLEGE
HONORS PROGRAM

Johnson County Community College provides a range of services to allow persons with disabilities to participate in educational programs and activities. If you desire support services, contact the Student Access Center (913) 4XX-XXXX, Ext. 3XXX, or TDD 4XX-XXXX.

DESCRIPTION OF HONORS CONTRACT

This Honors Contract MUST be taken concurrently with the following course:

Course Title: HIST 140 - United States History to 1877

(course allowing the contract)

Mentor: W————— Y—————

Hours Credit: 1

Student's Name: _____

In addition to satisfying the normal objectives/competencies of the course, the student must complete the following additional objectives to accomplish a higher level of scholastic work:

Choose Objective 1, 2, or 3.

Objective 1:

After successful completion of this Honors Contract, the student will be able

1. To identify and explain the various explanations for and historiographical schools of thought on the causes of the American Civil War.

2. To relate project topic to general developments in United States history.

3. To conduct library research in United States history.

4. To do required reading and research at a level higher than that ordinarily required in a United States history survey course.

5. To develop and demonstrate writing skills appropriate to the field of history.

HIST 140 5/23/xx

Objective 2

After successful completion of this Honors Contract, the student will be able

1. To explain and describe the various schools of thought and historiographical arguments over the causes of the American Revolution. This will include general ideology and motivations, as well as actual events.

2. To relate this project topic to general developments in United States history during this period.

3. To conduct library research about the history of the United States.

4. To do required reading and research at a level higher than ordinarily required in a United States history survey course.

Objective 3

After successful completion of this Honors Contract, the student will be able

1. To describe and explain how the national perception and historical interpretation of the Puritans and Puritanism changed from the views of Puritans and their contemporaries to historians today.

2. To relate this project topic to general developments in United States history during this period.

3. To conduct library research in United States history.

4. To do required reading and research at a level higher than ordinarily required in a United States history survey course.

Tasks:

1. Read eight different approved selections, varying in length from lengthy essays, several chapters, or short books, and be prepared to discuss the arguments made by the author(s).

2. Meet with the mentor and fellow honors students at least eight times during the semester.

3. Write seven brief historical analysis papers, each 350-400 words long.

4. (Optional at the instructor's request) Present the results of this honors work before a class or meeting.

HIST 140   5/23/xx

Schedule of Conferences:

The student will meet with the mentor at least eight times during the semester on the following days at the time indicated:

(NOTE: This schedule will be arranged after contracts are signed.)

Expectations:

1. The student will complete all the requirements of this contract at a level of academic excellence.

2. The mentor will have the opportunity of working with the student on a tutorial basis.

3. The student will achieve a more advanced understanding of the methods of history and of the area of United States history to be studied in this research.

Grading Criteria:

1. Attendance at all eight required meetings with the mentor.

2. Completion of all assignments required by this contract at a level of academic excellence.

NORTHEAST COMMUNITY COLLEGE

HONORS PROGRAM

Any Honors Program student who has a disability that may prevent him/her from fully demonstrating his/her abilities should contact the Honors Program Director to discuss if accommodations are available or possible to complete course requirements.

DESCRIPTION OF HONORS CONTRACT

Sem. _____ Yr. _____ Date _____

This Honors Contract may be taken concurrently OR sequentially with the following course:

COURSE TITLE: Heating Ventilation & Air Conditioning

COURSE NO.: AC 2010

MENTOR: P—— B———

CREDIT HOURS: 1

STUDENT: _____

NOTE: Due to the nature of the objective in this Honors Contract, off-campus work will be necessary every week to accomplish these tasks. One "Holds Harmless Agreement" will be signed that will be good for the entire semester of this Honors Contract.

In addition to satisfying the normal objectives/competencies of the course, a student must complete the following additional objectives to accomplish a higher level of scholastic work:

OBJECTIVES:

Upon successful completion of this course, the student will be able to install and perform checkup (including mechanical troubleshooting) on a HVAC system.

The following tasks will be performed by the student:

1. Install a HVAC system.

2. Perform checkup and troubleshooting mechanical problems on a HVAC system.

3. Troubleshoot electrical HVAC problems.

4. Complete a list of mechanical components of a HVAC system.

5. Complete a list of electrical components of a HVAC system.

Schedule of mentor/student conferences:

A student/mentor conference schedule will be agreed upon at the outset of this contract.

Mentor's Expectations:

To properly install and service a residential HVAC system working at 100% efficiency.

Criteria for evaluating the work:

The student will be graded on the quality and completeness of the required assignments and/or projects.

NORTHEAST COMMUNITY COLLEGE
HONORS PROGRAM

Any Honors Program student who has a disability that may prevent him/her from fully demonstrating his/her abilities should contact the Honors Program Director to discuss if accommodations are available or possible to complete course requirements.

DESCRIPTION OF HONORS CONTRACT

Sem. _____ Yr. _____ Date _____

This Honors Contract MUST be taken concurrently with the following course:

COURSE TITLE: Algebra & Trigonometry

COURSE NO.: Math 1200

MENTOR: J— M——

CREDIT HOURS: 1

STUDENT:_____

In addition to satisfying the normal objectives/competencies of the course, a student must complete the following additional objectives to accomplish a higher level of scholastic work:

OBJECTIVES:

The student must complete five (5) of the following tasks to accomplish a higher level of scholastic work. The student must apply trigonometric relationships to advanced applications involving right triangles. Students may use graphing utilities and/or computer programs in order to complete the following tasks.

The following tasks will be performed by the student:

1. Solve five (5) problems involving trigonometry of right triangles. Answer in writing detailed questions pertaining to the results.

2. Solve and graph five (5) applications of sinusoidal functions. Provide a written explanation of the application.

3. Graph composition of functions. Graph the composition trigonometric functions. Determine amplitude and period of each composition.

4. Vectors application. Solve five (5) oblique triangles with vectors.

5. Polar graphs. Using Mathlab program graph lemniscate, cardioid, three-leaved rose, Spiral of Archimedes. Graph cycloid, four-leaved rose, Spiral of Archimedes.

6. Graph inverse sine, cosine, tangent using Mathlab.

7. Select a mathematician or topic of your choice. Read and summarize in good form, your finding, his/her contributions, and your reactions.

Schedule of mentor/student conferences:

A student/mentor conference schedule will be agreed upon at the onset of this contract.

Mentor's Expectations:

I expect the student to meet with me once a week for approximately 30 minutes to report on progress and answer questions and to spend one to two hours each week working independently.

Criteria for evaluating the work:

A grade of A will be earned by satisfactory completion of all five objectives with a 90% or better. (A grade of 80% will earn a B).

Oklahoma City Community College
Contract for Honors Credit

Date:_____

Student's Name: _____ ID#: _____

Course Title and Number: _____

Course Section Number:_____

Semester (Fall   Spring   Summer) _____ Fiscal Year:_____

Instructor's Name: _____ Division:_____

Describe as fully as possible the additional work or project that this student must complete in order to earn "honors" credit for the course. After both student and instructor sign the contract, return it to the Honors Coordinator for final approval.

Student's Signature _____

Instructor's Signature _____

Approved by _____

Honors Coordinator _____

Date _____

PALM BEACH
COMMUNITY COLLEGE

HONORS PROGRAM
Term _____ Year _____

HONORS OPTION CONTRACT

CONTRACT PROPOSAL

PLEASE TYPE OR PRINT NEATLY.

Student Name: Last		First	MI	Student SS#

Student Address	City	State/Zip	Tel # ( )	Cumulative GPA: *ATTACH TRANSCRIPT*

Course #	Section #	Reference #	Course Title:	Cr. Hrs	Campus/MS# /

Instructor Name: Last	First	Adjunct ___ Full-Time ___

Title of Project: _____

_____

Description of Project *(Attach paper if more room is needed.):* _____

_____

_____

Instructor's explanation of how this project is over and above the regular course work in accordance with criteria on back of this contract: _____

_____

_____

I agree to do the above project in accordance with the Honors standards.

Approved by:

_____
Student Signature   Date

_____
Associate Dean or Honors Representative   Date

_____
Instructor Signature   Date

_____
Honors Coordinator   Date

PROJECT COMPLETION

Honors Project Completed and Accepted:
No _____ Yes _____

Final Course Grade Earned: _____

I certify the above-named student has satisfactorily completed the Honors Option Contract in this course, according to the standards of the Honors Program listed on the back of this contract and the Honors checklist.

Paper Approved By:

_____
Associate Dean or Honors Representative   Date

_____
Instructor Signature   Date

_____
Honors Coordinator   Date

MINIMUM DESIGN GUIDELINES FOR HONORS OPTION PROJECTS

The Honors Option Project must represent a scholarly endeavor over and above the normally expected curriculum of the course, and it must be fully described on the Honors Option Contract.

EXAMPLES OF "What Makes it Honors":

• Topics that are more advanced than regular course work.

• Research beyond normal course assignment.

• Critical thinking and extended analysis not required in regular course work.

HONORS PROJECT PROCEDURE

Students must have a **3.2 cumulative GPA** and 12 hours of college completed or a **3.3 high school GPA.** The instructor will attach a copy of student transcript to this contract.

The instructor in consultation with the student determines the project design.

Typed paper, minimum of 1200 words, free of typographical, spelling, grammar, and style errors with **Honors cover page** attached is *MANDATORY for **ALL PROJECTS**.*

The instructor should arrange to meet with the student throughout the term to check on progress, work out details, etc. Three or four meetings are suggested.

The student must give an oral presentation or a summary of the project to the class sometime during the semester.

HONORS PROJECT DEADLINES

1. Contract proposals must be in Honors Coordinator's office by MIDTERM.

2. Final draft of Honors paper with completed contract attached and Pay/Grade form, must be in the Honors Coordinator's office **before** LAST DAY OF THE TERM.

NO HONORS PROJECTS WILL BE ACCEPTED AFTER THE LAST DAY OF THE TERM.

Sample Cover Page for
HONORS OPTION PROJECT

Two Remarkable First Ladies:
Eleanor Roosevelt and Hillary Clinton

An Honors Option Project
For Fundamentals of Speech
SPC 1600 - 1091
Palm Beach Community College
Central Campus

In Partial Fulfillment of the
Honors Option Agreement
for K——— A———

PALM BEACH COMMUNITY COLLEGE
HONORS PROGRAM   HONORS OPTION CONTRACT

Term _____ Year _____

PLEASE TYPE OR PRINT NEATLY.

STUDENT NAME: Last _____ First _____ MI ____ Cumulative GPA _____ STUDENT ID NUMBER _____

COURSE NO. _____ Section # _____ Reference # _____ *ATTACH TRANSCRIPT* Course Title _____

INSTRUCTOR NAME _____ Division _____ Campus _____

TITLE OF PROJECT: _____

DESCRIPTION OF PROJECT (Attach paper if more room is needed.): _____

INSTRUCTOR'S explanation of how this project is over and above the regular course work in accordance with criteria on back of this contract: _____

I agree to do the above project in accordance with the Honors standards.

_____   _____   _____   _____
Student Signature   Date   Division Chair   Date

_____   _____   _____   _____
Instructor Signature   Date   Honors Coordinator   Date

Honors Project Completed and Accepted: NO _____ YES _____   Final Course Grade Earned: _____

I certify the above-named student has satisfactorily completed the Honors Option Contract in this course, according to the standards of the Honors Program listed on the back of this contract and the Honors Policies and Procedures Manual.

_____   _____   _____   _____
Instructor Signature   Date   Honors Coordinator   Date

_____   _____
Division Chair   Date

APPLICATION

CERTIFICATION

MINIMUM DESIGN GUIDELINES FOR HONORS OPTION PROJECTS

The Honors Option Project must represent a scholarly endeavor over and above the normally expected curriculum of the course, and it must be fully described on the Honors Option Contract.

EXAMPLES OF "What Makes It Honors":

<u>Topics</u> that are too advanced for presentations in regular course work.

<u>Research</u> beyond normal course assignment.

<u>Critical thinking and extended analysis</u> not required in regular course work.

<u>Creative project</u> beyond regular requirements of the course.

HONORS PROJECT PROCEDURE

The instructor in consultation with the student determines the project design.

Student must have a 3.2 cumulative GPA; the instructor will attach a copy of the student transcript to the contract.

Paper should be typed and a minimum of 1200 words, free of typographical, spelling, grammar, and style errors. Honors cover page must be attached.

The instructor should arrange to meet with the student throughout the term to check on progress, work out details, etc. Three or four meetings are suggested.

The student should present the project or a summary of the project to the class sometime during the semester.

HONORS PROJECT DEADLINES

1. Contract proposals must be in the Honors Coordinator's office by <u>MIDTERM</u>.

2. The final draft of the Honors Project/Paper with a completed contract must be in the Honors Coordinator's office by <u>LAST DAY OF CLASSES, IF POSSIBLE,</u> **OR** <u>LAST DAY OF FINALS</u>.

READING AREA COMMUNITY COLLEGE
HONORS PROGRAM
PROPOSAL FOR HONORS CREDIT BY CONTRACT

Student _____ Student # _____

Course <u>BUS 230 Business Law</u>_____ Section #_____

Professor _____ Term/Year _____

In addition to satisfying the standard course requirements, the student will satisfactorily complete the following work to receive honors credit. (Provide a summary of the proposal below and attach a separate sheet containing a detailed account.)

The student will submit a memorandum of law regarding the case of *Blumental v. Matthew Drudge, the Drudge Report, and America Online.* The memorandum will provide the following information:

1. Background information on the social impact of changing communication technologies,

2. Potential legal issues for the plaintiff and the defendants and possible arguments to support their respective positions,

3. Discussion of what issue the court may or may not decide and why.

4. Personal conclusions about the social and legal issues raised in this case.

Student's Signature _____**Date** _____

Professor's Approval _____**Date** _____

Division Chair Approval_____**Date** _____

Honors Committee Approval _____**Date** _____

REQUEST FOR HONORS CREDIT
(To be completed at the end of the semester by the professor)

The student has satisfactorily completed the work described above in addition to or in place of the standard course requirements and is qualified to receive an honors designation for this course.

Faculty's Signature _____Date _____

Registrar: This form is valid only if all signatures have been provided.

Proposal for Honors Credit by Contract

The *Blumenthal* case is a suitable project for this business law class because it raises several important legal and social issues. G—— T—— will need to do original research on the social and legal impact of previous revolutions in communications technology, and provide an analysis of what these previous adjustments may mean in the *Blumenthal* case. A discussion of possible political implications may also be appropriate.

She will be expected to discuss from both the plaintiff and defendant positions the following legal questions: Is America Online a publisher or merely a "newsstand" providing access to published information? Do the remarks made by Matthew Drudge in the *Drudge Report* fall under the protection of the Supreme Court's decision in *New York Times v. Sullivan* (a landmark decision in the publishing industry)? Does the medium, the Internet, have any bearing on what is or what should be the legal liability of America Online and Matthew Drudge?

The writing quality for the legal memorandum should meet the standard expected of first-year law students serving their first summer clerkship. G—— T—— will not be expected to provide a detailed legal analysis, but she will need to demonstrate the following: a fundamental understanding of the controlling legal principles in this case, how the plaintiff and the defendants will view these principles and apply them to their respective positions, and a knowledge of legal terminology and the ability to use it properly.

Citations for court cases will follow the standard legal format. All other citations will follow the MLA standard.

READING AREA COMMUNITY COLLEGE
HONORS PROGRAM
PROPOSAL FOR HONORS CREDIT BY CONTRACT

Student_____ Student #_____

Course <u>Abnormal Psychology</u> _____ Section # _____

Professor _____ Term/Year_____

In addition to satisfying the standard course requirements, the student will satisfactorily complete the following work to receive honors credit. (Provide a summary of the proposal below and attach a separate sheet containing a detailed account.)

The student will locate Internet websites that pertain to abnormal psychology and research the information to determine its validity. The websites will contain information that can be used as a reference by local social work/mental health organizations and students when writing research papers. A brief summary about each site will be written; its APA reference will also be provided.

Student's Signature_____ Date_____

Professor's Approval _____ Date_____

Division Chair Approval_____ Date_____

Honors Committee Approval _____ Date_____

REQUEST FOR HONORS CREDIT

(To be completed at the end of the semester by professor)

The student has satisfactorily completed the work described above in addition to or in place of the standard course requirements and is qualified to receive an honors designation for this course.

Faculty's Signature _____Date_____

Registrar: This form is valid only if all signatures have been provided.

The goal of this project is to find websites that contain valid information that can be used by human services organizations throughout the county as well as students needing resources for research papers. The websites will contain information covering the following topics: mental health (disorders, diagnoses, treatment, pharmacology, support groups, etc.), alcohol and drug abuse (self-help groups, treatment facilities, family member support groups), relationship/family conflict (problem solving, therapies, coping skills), domestic violence (women's shelters, counseling services, prevention), and developmental disabilities/mental retardation (support groups, group homes, job skills, life skills). These websites will then be added to websites being created for local human services agencies as a link providing additional information to people working within that agency or searching for a place to find help.

The student will evaluate each website found with information covering one of the above topics. The criteria to be used for evaluation will be authorship, publisher, sources used, and content. Additional help in establishing criteria and evaluation will come from the books *Online!* by Andrew Harnack and Eugene Kleppinger and *The Insider's Guide to Mental Health Resources Online* by John M. Grobol. The site should also be easy to browse and understand.

The timeline to be followed by the student is broken into four two-week sections with each section having a goal. The first goal shall be to perform basic research and become familiar with the information available on the Internet. Focusing on specific problems or topics is the second goal and will be followed by the third goal, which is to determine which sites are best for a certain topic. The last goal will be to summarize each website and document its APA reference. The instructor will conduct weekly evaluations of progress and information gathered.

HONORS CONTRACT

REDLANDS COMMUNITY COLLEGE

An honors contract is for additional and meritorious work completed in conjunction with the regular class. The in-depth honors study project should center on inquiry, discovery, and critical thinking. It should be a project above and beyond the normal requirements and expectations of the course.

Course Name and Number: Principles of Microeconomics 2203

Course Sequence Number: 2401

Semester and year course is to be offered: Spring 19xx

Student's name: _____

Instructor's name: _____

Check one of the following:

This course is a seminar _____.

This course is a general education requirement _____.

This course is a program requirement or elective _____.

Tasks to be performed by the student for fulfillment of the honors course requirements:

1. Student is to interview bank official(s) to research items such as educational requirements to be hired, chances for advancement, job satisfaction, etc.

2. Student is to make a written report to the instructor on the interview(s).

3. Student is to make an oral report to the entire class on the interview(s).

Above tasks should be completed no later than April 27, 19xx.

Student signature:_____Date: _____

Instructor signature:_____Date: _____

Honors Coordinator signature:_____Date: _____

Return this document to the Honors Program Coordinator before the third week of class for proper credit.

APPENDIX F

A Select Bibliography

This author again thanks William A. Senior of Broward Community College for permission to reprint with additions his previously published bibliography.

Achterberg, Cheryl. "The Ages of Imitation, Authenticity and Originality." *JNCHC* 6.1 (2005): 41-42.

——. "Differences between an Honors Program and Honors College." *JNCHC* 5.1 (2004): 87-96.

——. "Honors Assessment and Evaluation." *JNCHC* 7.1 (2006): 37-39.

——. "Honors in Research: Twenty Years Later." *JNCHC* 5.1 (2004): 33-36.

——. "Penn State Schreyer Honors College." *JNCHC* 3.2 (2002): 54.

——. "What Is an Honors Student?" *JNCHC* 6.1 (2005): 75-83.

Achterberg, Cheryl, Amanda Wetzel, and Emily Whitbeck. "Student-Led Quality Teams in the Classroom." *JNCHC* 3.1 (2002): 75-88.

Adler, Brian. "Having Intelligence with the Earth: The Greening of an Honors "Program." *Greening of the Campus III: Theory and Reality*. Ed. Robert J. Koester. Vol. 3. Muncie, IN: Ball State, 1999. 111-16.

Aievoli, Patrick. "Supporting the Aesthetic through Metaphorical Thinking." *JNCHC* 4.2 (2003): 89-99.

Albert, A. Midori, and Katherine E. Bruce. "Introducing the Video Web-board as a Technologic Enhancement to Your Honors Course." *JNCHC* 3.2 (2002): 33-44.

Andrews, Hans A., and Robert P. Marshall. "Challenging High School Honor Students with Community College Courses." *Community College Review* 19 (Summer 1991): 47-51.

Armstrong, A., et al. "Science Literacy and Religiosity: The Triangle Effect." *Forum for Honors* 21.2 (Summer/Fall 1992): 10-17.

Armstrong, William B., and Liane De Meo. *Honors Program Evaluation*. San Diego: San Diego Community College District, 1989.

Arnold, Thomas P., Francis A. Frierson, and Neil Sebacher, Jr. "An NIH-and NSF-Funded Program in Biological Research for Community College Students." *JNCHC* 1.2 (2000): 75-81.

Austin, C. Grey. "Honors Learning in the Seventies." *Educational Record* 56.3 (Summer 1975): 160-69.

——. *Honors Programs: Development, Review, and Revitalization*. NCHC Monographs in Honors Education. NCHC, 1991.

——. "Orientation to Honors Education." Friedman and Jenkins-Friedman 5-16.

—. "The Principles and Practices of Honors Education: An Overview." *Forum for Honors* 16.4 (Summer 1986).

Austin, C. Grey, et al. *Handbook for the Evaluation of an Honors Program.* National Collegiate Honors Council, 1981.

Bach, Betsy, Rachel Kinkie, and Sam Schabacker. "Using Student Mentors in an 'Introduction to Honors' Course." *HIP* 1 (2005): 139-145.

Badra, Robert, and Helen Palleschi. "Partnerships across the Disciplines: The Humanities, Science and Technology: Making Connections." Practicing Community Leadership: Partnerships are the Key to Success. 1993. ERIC ED358890.

Barloon, Sandra. "One Student's Perspective on the Iowa Honors Semester." *Forum for Honors* 20.3 (Winter/Spring 1991): 27-28.

Bass, Amy. "The Art of the Mash-up: Students in the Age of Digital Reproduction." *JNCHC* 6.1 (2005): 35-37.

Bateson, Myla. "Part Four: An Honors Philosophy." *National Honors Report* 15.2 (Summer 1994): 33-35.

Bell, James D. "Expand the Honors Curriculum: Teach Entrepreneurship, Risk-Taking, and Change Across the Curriculum." *HIP* 1 (2005): 93-101.

Berbiglia, Violeta A., Leslie Goddard, and John H. Littlefield. "Gaming: a Strategy for Honors Programs." *Journal of Nursing Education* 36.6 (1997): 289-91.

Berger, Helen A. "School as Text." *National Honors Report* 15.3 (Fall 1994): 28-30.

Blaich, Charles F., and Mauri A. Ditzler. "Creating a Common Voice for Liberal Arts Education." *JNCHC* 3.1 (2002): 27-30.

Blythe, Heather L. "Ethics on an Honors College Campus: An Analysis of Attitudes and Behaviors of Honors Students versus Non-Honors Students." *JNCHC* 5.2 (2004): 25-35.

Bolch, Kambra. "Contracting in Honors." *HIP* 1 (2005): 49-61.

Brabant, Margaret, and Anne M. Wilson. "Community Beyond Honors: Butler University's Community Fellows Program." *HIP* 2 (2006): 35-42.

Bradbard, Marilyn R., and Harriet Watkins Giles. "The Family, Consumer, and Nutritional Sciences Honors Program for Talented High School Students: An Auburn University Case Study." *Journal of Home Economics* 79 (Summer 1987): 23-27+.

Braid, Bernice. "The Age of False Positives." *JNCHC* 6.1 (2005): 25-27.

—. "Cultivating Too." *JNCHC* 2.1 (2001): 91-94.

—. "Honors as Nexus." *National Honors Report* 16.3 (Fall 1995): 63-67.

—. "Liberal Education and the Challenge of Intergrative Learning." *JNCHC* 1.1 (2000): 53-58.

—. "On Reflection." *Forum for Honors* 20.3 (Winter/Spring 1991): 4-18.

Braziller, Amy, and Chris Howell. "Red Rocks Community College." *JNCHC* 3.2 (2002): 55-56.

Brenneise, Coral A. ed. *Organization and Working Policy for the Andrews University Undergraduate Honors Program.* Berrien Springs, MI: Andrews U, 1992. ERIC ED341324. http://search.epnet.com/login.aspx?direct=true&db=eric&an=ED341324.

Brewton, Vince. "What Honors Can Do." *JNCHC* 6.2 (2005): 39-41.

Brown, Earl. "Do Honors Programs Make a Difference? Why Do We Care?" *Forum for Honors* 20.4 (Summer/Fall 1991): 28-36.

—. "Honors Admissions and Recruitment." *National Honors Report* 18.1 (Spring 1997): 4-6.

—. "So You Wanna Take an Honors Course." *National Honors Report* 12.4 (Winter 1992): 16-17.

—. "Teaching Teachers to Teach Honors." *National Honors Report* 13.4 (Winter 1993): 13-14.

Buckner, Ellen. "Honors Research in Nursing: Integration of Theory and Evidence-Based Practice using Multiple Modalities of Thinking." *JNCHC* 5.1 (2004): 53-60.

Buckner, Ellen B., and Cynthia Leach-Fuller. "Honors and the Creative Arts in Nursing: Music Therapy to Decrease Anxiety in Critical Care Patients." *JNCHC* 2.2 (2001): 77-82.

Bruffee, Kenneth A. "Knowledge Communities, Collaborative Learning, and Honors Education." *Forum for Honors* (Spring 1988).

—. "Making the Senior Thesis Work." *Forum for Honors* 21.3 (Spring/Summer 1993): 2-10.

—. "The Social Construction of Knowledge and the Future of Honors Education." *National Honors Report* 7.2 (Summer 1986): 1+.

Bulakowski, Carole, and Barbara K. Townsend. "Evaluation of a Community College Honors Program: Problems and Possibilities." *Community College Journal of Research and Practice* 19.6 (Nov./ Dec. 1995): 485-99.

Bush, Renee B, and Margaret R. Wells. "Bibliographic Instruction for Honors Students: The University at Buffalo Experience." *Research Strategies* 8.3 (Summer 1990): 137-43.

Byrne, Joseph P. "Honors Programs in Community Colleges: A Review of Recent Issues and Literature (ERIC Review)." *Community College Review* 26.2 (Fall 1998):67-81. ERIC EJ575937. http://search.epnet.com/login.aspx?direct=true&db=eric&an=EJ575937.

California State Colleges. Division of Academic Planning. *Proceedings of the Honors and Advanced Placement Conference.* Los Angeles, 1969.

Campbell, K. Celeste. "Allocation of Resources: Should Honors Programs Take Priority?" *JNCHC* 6.1 (2005): 95-103.

—. "The Perceived Value of Honors Works as It Relates to Faculty Promotion and Tenure." *JNCHC* 4.1 (2003): 13-25.

Carmody, Denise L. "Values in Honors Education." *National Honors Report* 10.3 (Fall 1989): 3-7.

Carnicom, Scott, and Michael Clump. "Assessing Learning Style Differences between Honors and Non-Honors Students." *JNCHC* 5.2 (2004): 37-43.

Carrafiello, Susan. "Wright State University." *JNCHC* 3.2 (2002): 58.

Carrish, Sharon. "Reviving an Honors Program with Specialized Sequence Tracks." *HIP* 1 (2005): 63-77.

Case, Robert P. "Honors: the Core Community in Higher Education." *National Honors Report* 15.1 (Spring 1994): 1-3.

—. "Honors and the Learning Process." *National Honors Report* 14.2 (Summer 1993): 8-10.

—. "Liberal Arts and Honors: New Direction and Convergent Paths." *National Honors Report* 13.2 (Summer 1992): 13-14.

Castro-Johnson, Malaika, and Alvin Y. Wang. "Emotional Intelligence and Academic Performance of College Honors and Non-Honors Freshmen." *JNCHC* 4.2 (2003): 105-14.

Charpie, John C., and Michael Shea. "Science and Writing (interdisciplinary [syllabus])." *HIP* 2 (2006): 129-133.

Clewitt, Rick. "The Honors Program Thesis: A Delineation of Issue and Advice Based on a Questionnaire." *Forum for Honors* 21.3 (Spring/Summer 1993): 11-17.

—. "Re-Thinking Non-Honors Courses." *National Honors Report* 15.2 (Summer 1994): 5-17.

Clewitt, Rick, and Bonnie Gray. "Varieties of Core Curricula in Honors Programs." *National Honors Report* 17.4 (Winter 1997): 27-32.

Clewitt, Rick, et al. "Grading and Teaching." *National Honors Report* 15.2 (Summer 1994): 19-26.

Cohen, A.M., and F.B. Brawer. *The American Community College.* 3rd ed. San Francisco: Jossey-Bass, 1997. See also Itawamba Community College, Exploring America's Communities. Fulton, MS: Itawamba Community College, 1996.

Cohen, Ira. "A Brief Disquisition on the Creation of Honors as a Recognized Field of and in Academe." *National Honors Report* 17.4 (Winter 1997): 19-20.

—. "Honors as Counterpoise." *National Honors Report* 12. 4 (Winter 1992): 1-4.

Cohn, Cheryl. "Student-Based Curriculum in Honors Seminars." *National Honors Report* 15.2 (Summer 1994): 46-48.

Community College Honor Programs: an ERIC Bibliography. Los Angeles: ERIC Clearinghouse for Junior Colleges, 1983.

Conway, Gertrude. "Honoring Freshmen: Assessing Needs and Setting Goals." *National Honors Report* 12.4 (Winter 1992): 23-24.

Conway, Jeremiah. "If We Honor Education, Freshmen Will Be Honored." *National Honors Report* 12.4 (Winter 1992): 21-23.

Cosgrove, John R. "The Impact of Honors Programs on Undergraduate Academic Performance, Retention, and Graduation." *JNCHC* 5.2 (2004): 45-53

Cottrill, Angela, and Robert T. Rhode. "In the Line of Fire: Honors Programs amid Ideological Battles." *Forum for Honors* 21.1 (Winter/Spring 1992): 3-11.

Cox, Mitch. "Revising the Literature Curriculum for a Pluralist Society. (Independent Reading in a Freshman Honors Class)." *English Journal* 77 (Oct. 1988): 30-34.

Crawford, M., E. Larsen, and L. Fitton. "Defining Success from the Honors Student's Point of View." *Forum for Honors* 21.4 (1993): 17-24.

Crooks, Steven M., and Susan G. Haag. "Evaluating a Community College Honors Program: Perceptions of Effectiveness and Value." *Community College Journal of Research and Practice* 18.5 (Sept/Oct 1994): 485-97.

Csokasy, Judie. "Curriculum as Praxis: An Honors Project for Nursing Students." *National Honors Report* 18.2 (Summer 1997): 10-12.

Culver, Robert, Emile Pilafidis, and Vijay Sathe. "Fusing Theory and Practice: Honors Consulting Projects for Drucker MBA Students." *Journal of Education for Business* 73.5 (May/June 1998): 298-301.

Cummings, Richard. "Basic Characteristics of a Fully-Developed Honors Program." *National Honors Report* 16.3 (Fall 1995): 20-21.

Cundall, Michael K., Jr. "How to Develop and Promote an Undergraduate Research Day." *HIP* 2 (2006): 49-57.

—. "Responsibility and Imitation." *JNCHC* 6.1 (2005): 39-40.

Daniel, William W., Jr. "Semesters and Virtuous Practice." *Forum for Honors* 20.3 (Winter/Spring 1991): 29-34.

Davy, Freddye T. "Cultural Considerations for Honors Programs." *National Honors Report* 16.3 (Fall 1995): 31-3.

Deckelbaum, David. "Honors Programs and Offerings in the Community Colleges." *Community College Journal of Research and Practice* 18.2 (Mar./April 1994): 215-19.

DeSalva, Joy, and Nathan P. Ritchey. "The University Scholars Program: A Case Study in the Recruitment and Retention of High-Caliber Students." *College and University* 71.4 (Spring 1996): 21-25.

De Sevo, Margaret. "Honor in Nursing: A Work in Progress." *National Honors Report* 18.2 (Summer 1997): 27-29.

Digby, Joan. "The Age of Imitation." *JNCHC* 6.1 (2005): 17-24.

—. "Further Thoughts on the Future of NCHC." *JNCHC* 2.1 (2001): 73-75.

—. "Long Island University, C.W. Post Campus." *JNCHC* 3.2 (2002): 50-51.

—. "They Graduated." *JNCHC* 7.1 (2006): 57-59.

Digby, Joan, and Tracey Christy. "Keeping Honors Information Current." *HIP* 1 (2005): 17-19.

Donovan, Leslie A. "Jesters Freed from their Jack-in-the-Boxes: Or Springing Creativity Loose from Traditionally Entrenched Honors Students." *JNCHC* 2.2 (2001): 93-103.

Douglas, P., et al. "Factors in the Choice of Higher Education Institutions by Academically Gifted Seniors." *Journal of College Student Personnel* 24 (1983): 540-45.

Drueke, Tim. "Graduates' Perceptions of the University of Nebraska-Lincoln Honors Program." *National Honors Report* 17.1 (Spring 1996): 18-23.

—. "Graduates' Perceptions of the University of Nebraska-Lincoln Honors Program." *National Honors Report* 17.2 (Summer 1996): 10-19.

Dudley, Charles J. "Breaking the Rules: University Honors and the Curriculum. "*National Honors Report* 15.3 (Fall 1994): 51-53.

Dunn, Dana S, and Lori J. Toedter. "The Collaborative Honors Project in Psychology: Enhancing Student and Faculty Development." *Teaching of Psychology* 18 (Oct 1991): 178-80.

Edman, Laird R. O., and Sally Oakes Edman. "Emotional Intelligence and the Honors Student." *JNCHC* 5.2 (2004): 15-24.

England, James. "External Examiners Assess Honors Students." *Liberal Education* 73 (May/June 1987): 32-33.

Estess, Ted L. "Books, Books, Books." *JNCHC* 1.1 (2000): 10-17.

—. "Honors Scholarship: Another View." *JNCHC* 5.1 (2004): 25-27.

Etheridge, Sandra Y. "Honors: Getting Started." *National Honors Report* 13.2 (Summer 1992): 7-12.

Evans, Chris, et al. "Creating a Neighborhood in an Honors Program: A Commitment to the Community." *National Honors Report* 17.3 (Fall 1996): 17-20.

Evans, Robert. "The Meaning of 'Research' for Honors: What Do We Really Want to Know?" *National Honors Report* 8.4 (Winter 1987): 1-4.

Fischer, David. "The New Honors Programs." *US News and World Report* 16 Sept. 1996: 108-10.

Fleishman, Sylvia Saari, and Thomas E. Furlong, Jr. "Honors Programs in the Florida Community College System." *Visions: The Journal of Applied Research for the Florida Association of Community Colleges* 2.2 (Summer 1999): 33-37.

Fosnight, Stephanie Renee. "When Austen's Heroines Meet: a Play in One Act." *JNCHC* 2.2 (2001): 113-36.

Franson, Margaret. "'The Play's the Thing': Theater Arts and Liberal Learning." *JNCHC* 2.2 (2001): 21-25.

Freeman, Mabel G. "An Honors Living/Learning Center: What's Involved?" *National Honors Report* 8.4 (Winter 1987): 7-8.

Freyman, Jay. "What is an Honors Student?" *JNCHC* 6.2 (2005): 23-29.

—. "When It's Bad Cess to Assess!" *JNCHC* 7.1 (2006): 41-42.

Friedman, Paul G., and Reva C. Jenkins-Friedman, eds. *Fostering Academic Excellence through Honors Programs.* New Directions for Teaching and Learning. 25. San Francisco: Jossey-Bass, 1986.

Frost, Linda. "Saving Honors in the Age of Standardization." *JNCHC* 7.1 (2006): 21-25.

Fuller, John R., and David Wagner. "The Honors Trip." *National Honors Report* 13.4 (Winter 1993): 31-32.

Gabelnick, Faith. "Curriculum Design: the Medium is the Message." Friedman and Jenkins-Friedman 75-86.

—. "Honors Semesters as Learning Communities: Designing New Kinds of Syntheses." *Forum for Honors* 20.3 (Winter/Spring 1991): 19-26.

—. "Leading and Learning in Community." *JNCHC* 1.1 (2000): 42-52.

Ghosh, Jayati, M. Patricia Dougherty, and Kenneth Porada. "Dominican University of California's Honors Program and its Relation to University Heritage and Mission." *HIP* 2 (2006): 27-32.

Gillen, Francis. "A Unique Brochure: Honors at the University of Tampa." *National Honors Report* 12.4 (Winter 1992): 6-11.

Gillison, Linda Rutland. "Presidential Scholars, Plato & Politics." *National Honors Report* 18.4 (Winter 1998): 26-29.

Glaze, Eliza, and Philip Whalen. "East Meets West (interdisciplinary [syllabus])." *HIP* 2 (2006): 117-20.

Godow, Rew A., Jr. "Honors Program Leadership: The Right Stuff," *Forum for Honors* 16.3 (Spring 1986): 3-9.

Gordon, V.V. "Meeting the Career Development Needs of Undecided Honors Students." *Journal of College Student Personnel* 24 (1983): 82-83.

Grangaard, Daniel R. "Personality Characteristics and Favorite Topics of Students Enrolled in Introduction to Psychology, Honors." *JNCHC* 4.1 (2003): 41-52.

Green, Deborah. "Getting Honors Level Work Out of Your Honors Students." *National Honors Report* 18.4 (Winter 1998): 43-44.

Greenspan, Anders. "Design and Deception at Colonial Williamsburg." *JNCHC* 3.1 (2002): 61-66.

Greer, Richard M., Retta E. Poe, and Randi Sugarman. "A Career Education Workshop for Honors Students: a Student Affairs/Academic Affairs Collaboration." *Journal of College Student Development* 38 (May/June 1997): 303-5.

Grier, David Alan. "A Note on Honors Admission and the SAT." *National Honors Report* 18.2 (Summer 1997): 2-5.

—. "Tenets, Standards, and Emerging Paradigms." *National Honors Report* 16.3 (Fall 1995): 21-23.

—. "Two Days to a Better Honors Program: Unifying the Student Community and Improving Critical Thinking with a Short Symposium." *National Honors Report* 17.1 (Spring 1996): 10-13.

Gross, David, and Craig Womack. "The Academic Habit: A Unique Co-Curricular-based Honors Course." *National Honors Report* 14.2 (Summer 1993): 27-30.

Guerrero, Janis K., and Shelley A. Riggs. "The Preparation and Performance of Freshmen in University Honors Programs: A Faculty Perspective." *Journal of Secondary Gifted Education* 8.1 (Fall 1996): 41-48.

Guzy, Annmarie. "Faculty Compensation and Course Assessment in Honors Composition." *JNCHC* 5.1 (2004): 105-14.

—. *Honors Composition: Historical Perspectives and Contemporary Practices.* National Collegiate Honors Council. 2003.

—. "Originality Is a Risk." *JNCHC* 6.1 (2005): 29-30.

—. "Research in Honors and Composition." *JNCHC* 5.1 (2004): 37-39.

Haas, Paul F. "Honors Programs: Applying the Reflective Judgment Model." *Liberal Education* 78.1 (Jan./Feb. 1992): 20-23.

Hahn, Leslie, and Jim Rogers. "Cultural Enrichment: Finding Where You Fit, Exploring Individuality and Community (1-hour introductory course [syllabus)." *HIP* 2 (2006): 111-15.

Hall, Cheryl Jackson. "Role Playing and Simulation in a Course on Vietnam and the Sixties." *National Honors Report* 15.3 (Fall 1994): 5-17.

Harte, Thomas B. "Honors and Non-Honors Students: How Different Are They?" *National Honors Report* 15.2 (Summer 1994): 12-14.

Hartleroad, Gayle E. "Comparison of the Academic Achievement of First-Year Female Honors Program and Non-Honors Program Engineering Students." *JNCHC* 6.2 (2005): 109-20.

Harvey, Maria Luisa Alvarez. "Minorities and Women and Honors Education." Friedman and Jenkins-Friedman 41-51.

Hawthorne, Jill M., and Gary D. Malaney. "Helping High School Scholars Adjust to a Large, Public Research University: an Evaluation of a Two-Day Orientation to the Honors Program." *College and University* 67 (Summer 1992): 257-62.

Heck, Jim. "Model for Community College Honors Programs." *Community College Review* 13 (Summer 1985): 46-9.

Herbert, Jim. "On Discourse." *JNCHC* 1.1 (2000): 73-74.

Herr, Norman Edward. "Administrative Policies Regarding Advanced Placement and Honors Coursework." *NASSP Bulletin* 76.5 (May 1992): 80-87.

—. "A Comparative Analysis of the Perceived Influence of Advanced Placement and Honors Programs upon Science Instruction." *Journal of Research in Science Teaching* 29.5 (May 1992): 521-32.

—. "The Influence of Program Format on the Professional Development of Science Teachers: Teacher Perception of AP and Honors Science Courses." *Science Education* 75.6 (Nov 1991): 619-29.

—. "National Curricula for Advanced Science Classes in American High Schools? The Influence of the College Board's Advanced Placement Program on Science Curricula." *International Journal of Science Education* 15 (May/June 1993): 297-306.

Herron, Laura Bender. "Redemptive Memory: The Christianization of the Holocaust in America." *JNCHC* 6.2 (2005): 61-91.

Hickson, R.H., and J.C. Driskill. "Need for Achievement: Differences between Honors and Non-Honors Students." *The Journal of Experimental Education* 38 (1970): 37-8.

Hill, James P. "What Honors Students Want (And Expect): The Views of Top Michigan High School and College Students." *JNCHC* 6.2 (2005): 95-107.

Hiltner, Judith. "Learning Curves: Fieldwork as Context for Interrogating the Dynamics of Work in American Culture." *JNCHC* 4.1 (2003): 63-83.

Hogner, Robert H. "Interdisciplinary Honors Teaching: Inquiry, Teaching, and Service as Holistic Activity." *National Honors Report* 16.3 (Fall 1995): 59-63.

Holland, Robert M. "Self-Reorientation to an Honors Program: An Anonymous Questionnaire." *National Honors Report* 13.2 (Summer 1992): 25-26.

Homan, Paul. "A Humanist in Honors: Another Look at Catherine Cater." *JNCHC* 1.2 (2000): 87-90.

"Honors Programs." (Symposium.) *Engineering Education* 76 (Nov. 1985): 85-96.

Honors Programs in American Colleges and Universities, Index. Boulder, CO: National Collegiate Honors Council, 1967.

"Honors Programs in the Community, Technical, and Junior College." (Symposium.) *Community, Technical, and Junior College Journal* 58 (Apr./May 1988): 26-32.

"Honors Programs and Offerings in the Community Colleges." (ERIC Report.) *Community College Journal of Research and Practice* 18 (Mar./Apr. 1994): 215-19.

Hood, Connie K. "The Care and Feeding of Peer Mentors." *National Honors Report* 17.3 (Fall 1996): 9-12.

Horne, David Lawrence. "Ethnic Minorities and Modern Honors Programs: A Pragmatic Nexus." *National Honors Report* 10.1 (Spring 1989): 7-8.

Huelin, Scott. "The Promise, Perils, and Practices of Multiperspectivism." *JNCHC* 4.2 (2003): 21-26.

Huggett, Kathryn Dey. "Fostering Microenvironments for Teaching and Learning: Findings of a Study of Program Quality in Honors Programs." *JNCHC* 4.2 (2003): 53-88.

Innovations in Honors Programs. Spurrier, Robert L., and Natalie Bruner. Videocassette. Stillwater, Okla.: Oklahoma State University Television Services, 1994.

Innovations in Undergradute Research and Honors Education: Proceedings of the Second Schreyer National Conference. Ed. Josephine M. Carubia and Renata S. Engel. Ames, IA: National Collegiate Honors Council, 2004.

Inouye, Jillian. "A Research Development Program for Minority Honors Students." *Journal of Nursing Education* 34 (Sept. 1995): 268-71.

Irwin, Bonnie D. "A Student like Me." *JNCHC* 6.2 (2005): 53-54.

Jackson, Jocelyn Whitehead. "The Growth of Honors Programs in Small and Community Colleges." Friedman and Jenkins-Friedman 65-74.

Jahnke, C.L. "A Comparative Survey of Honors Programs and Non-Honors Program Graduates." *Forum for Honors* 8.2 (1977): 28-44.

James, Theresa A. *A Handbook for Honors Programs at Two-Year Colleges.* Lincoln: National Collegiate Honors Council, 2006.

Jenkins-Friedman, Reva C. "Identifying Honors Students." Friedman and Jenkins-Friedman 29-40.

Jernigan, Rosemary. "Creating a Stampede for the Community College Honors Program." *National Honors Report* 15.3 (Fall 1994): 23-24.

Kallendorf, Hilaire. "Let's Hear It From the Students: The Ideal Honors Class." *National Honors Report* 15.1 (Spring 1994): 39-42.

Kelleher, Jacqueline P. "Honors: When Value-Added is Really Added Value." *JNCHC* 6.2 (2005): 55-58.

Kelly, James S. "*Collaborative Learning: Higher Education, Interdependence, and the Authority of Knowledge* by Kenneth Bruffee: A Critical Study." *JNCHC* 3.1 (2002): 91-100.

Kennedy, Ellen J. "Term Limits for Honors Directors." *National Honors Report* 17.1 (Spring 1996): 3-4.

Kennedy, Ellen J., and David Rounds. "Business in Fiction." *National Honors Report* 15.2 (Summer 1994): 48-52.

Khé, Sriram. "A Way of Life." *JNCHC* 6.2 (2005): 47-48.

Khoon, Koh Aik, R. Abd-Shukor, and Sharifah Barlian Aidid. "Some Observations on Students' Honors Theses—Lessons for Future Generations." *College Student Journal* 29 (March 1995): 12-15.

Kish, Evelyn Rubio, and Emilio Santa Rita. "The Minority Honors Program in Energy-Related Curricula." *College and University* 68.2 (1993): 80-85. ERIC EJ467220.

Kitchell, Kenneth. "Honors on Trial: Letting Students into the Loop." *National Honors Report* 16.1 (Spring 1995): 16-19.

Knauer, James T. "Honors and Elitism: Oligarchy or Democracy?" *Forum for Honors* 21.1 (Winter/Spring 1992): 25-37.

Knobel, Dale. "Liberal Education: 'Learning to Learn.'" *JNCHC* 3.1 (2002): 19-22.

Kolmerten, Carol. "Learning and Research with Students: The Example of the Tilton/Beecher Scandal." *JNCHC* 1.1 (2000): 59-72.

Krasne, Betty. "Community and Individuality, Security and Risk: The Delicate Balance." *Forum for Honors* 20.2 (Summer/Fall 1990): 20-28.

—. "On Neutral Ground: A Practicum in Field-Based Learning." *Forum for Honors* 20.3 (Winter/Spring 1991): 29-38.

—. "Telling Tales Out of School: Academic Novels and Memoirs by Women." *JNCHC* 2.1 (2001): 27-39.

Kreith, Frank, and Jeremiah M. Allen, eds. *Honors Programs in Engineering: Report of the Conference Sponsored by the National Science Foundation at the University of Colorado, Boulder, Colorado, June 10-14, 1963.* Boston: Allyn and Bacon, 1964.

Kruer, Matthew. "'A Country Wonderfully Prepared for their Entertainment': The Aftermath of the New England Indian Epidemic of 1616." *JNCHC* 4.1 (2003): 85-103.

Kuwahara, Yasue. "Popular Culture Studies and Honors Learning." *National Honors Report* 14.2 (Summer 1993): 23-26

Labinger, Andrea. "Fostering Community and Maintaining Integrity in Honors Education." *National Honors Report* 15.1 (Spring 1994): 34-38.

Labinger, Andrea, et al. "The Nuts and Bolts of Honors Advising." *National Honors Report* 17.3 (Fall 1996): 13-16.

Lacey, Jim. "Honors Courses: More Difficult or Different?" *HIP* 1 (2005): 79-83.

Lane, Jennifer. "The Impact of K-12 Gifted Programs on Postsecondary Honors Programming." *JNCHC* 7.1 (2006): 63-73.

Lang, Andrew, Aimee Raile, and Joy Thrall. "A Multi-Perspective Class Project at Oral Roberts University." *JNCHC* 4.2 (2003): 101-03

Larsen, William L. "Honors Programs in Engineering: a Waiting Opportunity."*Engineering Education* 76 (Nov. 1985): 89-92.

Laubenbacher, Reinhard C, and David J. Pengelley. "Honors Mathematics in the Liberal Arts Curriculum." *National Honors Report* 10.2 (Summer 1989): 21-22.

Lawrence, Jane. "Honors Programs within Multi-Campus Systems: Opportunities for Cooperation and Collaboration." *National Honors Report* 15.1 (Spring 1994): 4-5.

—. "Moving in Honors." *National Honors Report* 16.3 (Fall 1995): 28-30.

Lawrence, Jane Fiori, and Lorine Potts-Dupre. "Collaborative Teaching and Learning: Essential to Honors Programs." *National Honors Report* 10.2 (Summer 1989): 13-16.

Laws, Page R. "Media Literacy and Liberation: Honors Students as Prophetic Artists and Critics." *JNCHC* 2.2 (2001): 27-41.

LeRoy, Karen, and Donald Morales. "Representing Reality: A Multi-Disciplinary Honors Program." *National Honors Report* 16.2 (Summer 1995): 39-41.

Levitan, Herbert. "Grant Support from the National Science Foundation to Improve Undergraduate Education for All Students in Science and Mathematics, Engineering and Technology." *JNCHC* 1.2 (2000): 65-74.

Levy, Diane. "The Shock of the Strange, the Shock of the Familiar: Learning from Study Abroad." *JNCHC* 1.1 (2000): 75-83.

Link, Ron. "The Pitfalls of Honors Programs." *Community, Technical, and Junior College Journal* 58 (Apr/May 1988): 27-28.

Lockwood, Linda G. "Is the Ivy Metaphor Appropriate for Honors?" *National Honors Report* 10.3 (Fall 1989): 7-8.

Long, Ada. *A Handbook for Honors Administrators.* National Collegiate Honors Council, 1995.

Longo, Peter J., and John Falconer. "Diversity Opportunities for Higher Education and Honors Programs: A View from Nebraska." *JNCHC* 4.1 (2003): 53-61.

Lopez, L. Luis. "Could Aristotle Teach the Honors Courses I Envision? Theory and Practice in the Arts." *JNCHC* 2.2 (2001): 73-76.

Lopez, Ramon E. "An Interdisciplinary Undergraduate Space Physics Course." *Journal of College Science Teaching* 25 (Feb. 1996): 263-69.

López-Chávez, Celia. "Teaching 'The Other Legacy,' Learning About Ourselves: Latin America in Honors." *JNCHC* 3.1 (2002): 67-74.

Lovata, Troy R. "The Legacy of Ancient Technology (social science [syllabus])." *HIP* 2 (2006): 125-28.

Lucas, John, et al. *Follow-Up Study of Students Taking Honors Courses, 1990-95.* Palatine, IL: William Rainey Harper C, 1995. ERIC ED397904.

Machonis, Peter. "Overview of the NCHC Faculty Institute in Miami and the Everglades." *HIP* 2 (2006): 103.

Mack, Maynard, Jr. "These Things Called Honors Programs." *Liberal Education* 82.2 (Spring 1996): 34-39.

Mack, Pam. "Clemson University." *JNCHC* 3.2 (2002): 46.

Madden, John D. "What is an Honors College?" *National Honors Report* 15.2 (Summer 1994): 5-40.

Magner, Denise K. "Honors Academy in Arizona Aims to Give Students 'a sense of international mission.'" *The Chronicle of Higher Education* 37 (July 31 1991): A23.

Major, John. "The Semester as Text." *Forum for Honors* 20.3 (Winter/Spring 1991): 39-42.

Malan, Leon C., Judith Muyskens, Anne Ponder, and Ann Page Steckler. "Leading a College as a Liberal Arts Practice." *JNCHC* 1.1 (2000): 18-31.

Malpezzi, Frances M. "Building a City of Ladies with Christine de Pizan and Arkansas State University Honors Students." *JNCHC* 7.1 (2006): 93-100.

Mandt, Jay. "Imitation, Economic Insecurity, and Risk Aversion." *JNCHC* 6.1 (2005): 43-45.

Mann, Sharlene. *The University-Wide Honors Program at the University of Arizona: The First Twenty-Two Years.* Tucson: U. of Arizona, 1984.

Mariz, George. "Accountable to Whom? Assessment for What?" *JNCHC* 7.1 (2006): 43-45.

—. "Full Circle: The Reappearance of Privelege and Responsibility in American High Education." *JNCHC* 2.1 (2001): 13-25.

—. "Western Washington University." *JNCHC* 3.2 (2002): 57.

—. "Women in Honors Education: The Case of Western Washington University." *JNCHC* 5.2 (2004): 87-100.

Massey, James. "Rhode is Right! Disconnectedness and the Honors Freshman." *National Honors Report* 14.4 (Winter 1994): 12-14.

—. "Rhode is Right, Part II: A Note on the Mesostructure of Honors Education." *National Honors Report* 15.2 (Summer 1994): 7-11.

Mathiason, R.E. "Characteristics of College Honors Students." *Journal of College Student Personnel* 26 (1985): 171-73.

Mayberry, Lillian F., and Jack Bristol. "An NSF-Funded Opportunity for Pre-Service Science Teachers." *JNCHC* 1.2 (2000): 83-85.

McCabe, Diann A. "Bringing Imagination into the Community through a Poetry-Writing Honors Course." *JNCHC* 2.2 (2001): 43-46.

McCarron, Bill. "Incorporating Film into the Honors English Classroom." *National Honors Report* 14.2 (Summer 1993): 21-23.

McCombs, Virginia. "Ten Things I Wish I Had Known as a New Honors Director." *National Honors Report* 18.4 (Winter 1998): 14-16.

McCoy, Claire Black. "Longwood University." *JNCHC* 3.2 (2002): 52.

McDermott, Don. "College Honors Programs Foster Elitism and Threaten Morale." *The Chronicle of Higher Education* 35 (Feb. 22 1989): B2. Reprinted *National Honors Report* 10.2 (Summer 1989): 7-8.

McGinley, Mark A. "Transferring a Course Developed for Honors Students to Non-Major Biology Students: Lessons Learned." *HIP* 1 (2005): 85-91.

McWenie, Megan. "Seeing Nature: Ansel Adams in the Human and Natural Environments of Yosemite." *JNCHC* 6.1 (2005): 57-71.

Menis, Donna M., and Robert P. Case. "Beginning in Honors: Approaching Basic Characteristics from a Small College Perspective." *National Honors Report* 18.1 (Spring 1997): 42-44.

Merline, Anne Marie. "Creating a Culture of Conducive Communication in Honors Seminars." *JNCHC* 5.2 (2004): 81-85.

Meyer, Arlin G. "Building Community in Honors Programs." *National Honors Report* 10.1 (Spring 1989): 10-11.

Miller, Kay, et al. "Corporate Culture and Honors Programs." *National Honors Report* 17.2 (Summer 1996): 3-9.

Minick, Theresa A., and Victoria Bocchicchio. "An Honors Pilot Course: Cross-Cultural Service and Inquiry-Based Learning in Mérida, Mexico." *HIP* 2 (2006): 59-69.

Moffett, Catherine, et al. "Honors Students in a Professional School: Perceived Needs and Goals." *National Honors Report* 15.1 (Spring 1994): 11-14.

Molledahl, Anne. "A Student's Perspective." *National Honors Report* 14.2 (Summer 1993): 7-8.

Montgomery, J.P. "Honors: Ghoulish Misconceptions." *National Honors Report* 18.1 (Spring 1997): 2-3.

Moran, Michael G. "Frank Aydelotte, Oxford University, and the Thought Movement in America." 1992 ERIC ED 344230.

Morgan, Joan. "Moving Beyond Retention to Academic Excellence." *Black Issues in Higher Education* 10 (Jan. 27 1994): 52+.

Morse, Joe, and Don Tucker. "Science and Mathematics in Honors: Why? How? How Much?" *National Honors Report* 17.1 (Spring 1996): 27-30.

Motlow State Community College. ""Exploring America's Communities: Honors American Studies. Progress Report." 1997. ERIC ED403951.

Mullins, Dail W., Jr. "A Biochemist in Honors." *JNCHC* 1.2 (2000): 21-29.

—. "The Science Education Crisis and Existential Apprehension." *Forum for Honors* 21.3 (Spring/Summer 1993): 18-31.

—. "Science Literacy and the Undergraduate Science Curriculum: Is It Time to Try Something Different?" *JNCHC* 2.1 (2001): 53-65.

—. "Teaching Science with a Single Equation." *National Honors Report* 18.2 (Summer 1997): 7-9.

—. "What is Honors?" *JNCHC* 6.2 (2005): 19-22.

—. "A Wing and A Prayer: Trying to Reinvent Undergraduate Science Education with an Honors Program Experiment." *National Honors Report* 15.3 (Fall 1994): 18-23.

New Freeland, Lisa. "Fun and Games of Teaching: Simulations in a Social Problems Course." *HIP* 2 (2006): 85-96.

Nichols, John. "The 'Little House' That Can." *JNCHC* 3.1 (2002): 31.

Nickolai, Bebe. "In Praise of Silence." *JNCHC* 6.2 (2005): 49-51.

—. "Writing and American Rhetoric (humanities [syllabus])." *HIP* 2 (2006): 135-39.

North Central Association of Colleges and Schools (U.S.). Council on Research and Service. *Honors Programs in the North Central Region.* Boulder, CO: The Association, 1978.

Ochs, Joy. "'You're Not Typical Professors, Are You?': Reflections on the NCHC Faculty Institute in Miami and the Everglades." *HIP* 2 (2006): 105-08.

Olivas, Michael A. *A Statistical Portrait of Honors Programs in Two-Year Colleges.* Washington: American Association of Community and Junior Colleges, 1975.

Orth, Geoffrey. "Funding Honors Needs through Student Government Resources." *HIP* 1 (2005): 39-40.

Osborne-Martin, Erin. "Understanding Caesar's Ethnography: A Contextual Approach to Protohistory." *JNCHC* 3.1 (2002): 39-58.

Ostrander, Tammy. "The Evolution of Aesthetic Response in Honors Students." *JNCHC* 2.2 (2001): 105-10.

Otero, Rosalie C. "Tenure and Promotion in Honors." *HIP* 1 (2005): 21-26.

—. "That Fine Little House." *JNCHC* 3.1 (2002): 23-26.

—. "What Honors Students are Like Now." *JNCHC* 6.1 (2005): 51-53.

Otero, Rosalie, and Robert Spurrier. *Assessing and Evaluating Honors Programs and Honors Colleges: A Practical Handbook*. Lincoln, NE: National Collegiate Honors Council, 1995.

Outcalt, C. L. "Community College Honors Programs: An Overview." 1999. ERIC ED427798

—. "Community College Honors Programs: A Digest from the ERIC Clearinghouse for Community Colleges." 1999. ERIC ED427798. http://www.gseis.ucla.edu/ERIC/ERIC/eric.html.

Palmer, A.B., and J. Wohl. "Some Personality Characteristics of Honors Students." *College Student Journal* 6 (1972): 106-11.

Patterson, David. "On the Image and Essence of Honors: Student, Professor, Program." *Forum for Honors* 20.2 (Summer/Fall 1990): 3-10.

—. "The Politically Correct Curriculum: A Desecration of Education." *Forum for Honors* 21.1 (Winter/Spring 1992): 18-24.

Payne, Brian K., et al. "Honor Research on Honors Students: a Collaboration." *National Honors Report* 18.1 (Spring 1997): 26-30.

Pehlke, Joy. "The Myth of an Honors Education." *JNCHC* 4.2 (2003): 27-33.

Peterson, John. "If I Had My Way, an Honors Program Would Look Like This." *National Honors Report* 7.2 (Summer 1986): 15-16.

Peterson's Smart Choices: Honors Programs & Colleges. Ed. Joan Digby. New York: Thomson Peterson's, 2005

Phillips, Greg. "The Role of Community College Honors Programs in Reducing Transfer Shock." *JNCHC* 5.1 (2004): 97-104.

Piehl, Mel. "The Hopes and Fears of Post-9/11 Years." *JNCHC* 6.1 (2005): 47-49.

Pienta, Norbert J., Craig Regitz, and Joseph Richards. "Curriculum and Experiments in an Organic Honors Laboratory: a Model for Parallel Honors and Regular Sections." *Journal of Chemical Education* 70 (Oct. 1993): 841-43.

Piland, William E., and Janet Azbell. "Atypical Profile: the Honors Program Student." *Community and Junior College Journal* 54 (Apr. 1984): 45-47.

Piland, William E., Patricia McKeague, and Warren Montgomery. "Serving Academically Gifted Students in Community Colleges." *The College Board Review* 143 (Spring 1987): 20-23+.

Piland, William E., et al. "Preferred Learning Styles and Teaching Strategies in the Honors Classroom." *Community/Junior College Quarterly of Research and Practice* 14.3 (Jul/Sept 1990): 227-37.

Pinti, Daniel. "Is, Ought, and Honors." *JNCHC* 6.2 (2005): 43-45.

Place as Text: Approaches to Active Learning. Ed. Bernice Braid and Ada Long. National Collegiate Honors Council, 2000.

Poremski, Karen M. "Stetson University (Collaborative Approach Helps Non-science Students)." *Liberal Education* 74 (Mar./Apr. 1988): 30-31.

Portnoy, Jeffrey A. "Business and Educational Values." *JNCHC* 7.1 (2006): 47-51.

—. "Cultivating Honors Excellence in the Other Garden." *JNCHC* 2.1 (2001): 83-85.

—. "Intimations of Imitation: Honors Students and their Alps." *JNCHC* 6.1 (2005): 31-34.

Powell, Brenda J. "A Director's Perspective." *National Honors Report* 14.2 (Summer 1993): 1-7.

Pressler, Jana L., Eric Rosenfeld, and Marianne Alverbo Larsson. "Stockholm Study Abroad: Scientific Breakthroughs and Nobel Laureates." *HIP* 1 (2005): 109-120.

Pruett, Dave. "Great Questions That Have Changed the World (science [syllabus])." *HIP* 2 (2006): 121–24.

Raia, Ann. "Honors Semesters Goals: A Working Draft." *Forum for Honors* 20.3 (Winter/Spring 1991): 67-73.

Ragin, Camilla. "Students Only: Teaching a Seminar on the Holocaust." *National Honors Report* 17.3 (Fall 1996): 33-34.

Rakow, Susan R. "Young-Adult Literature for Honors Students?" *English Journal* 80.1 (Jan. 1991): 48-51.

Randall, Catherine J., et al. "Honors Students as 'Prometheans.'" *Forum for Honors* 20.2 (Summer/Fall 1990): 29-34.

Randall, Cathy. "The Computer-Based Honors Program at the University of Alabama." *JNCHC* 3.2 (2002): 45.

Randall, Cathy, and Shay Copeland. "Are Honors Students Different." *Forum for Honors* (Fall/Winter 1986-7): 46-52.

Rawls, Diane, and Rosalie Otero. "Beyond the Bell-Curve: the Value of Teaching in Honors for Faculty." *National Honors Report* 17.1 (Spring 1996): 5-7.

Reed, Daisy F. "Honors Programs in Teacher Education." *Action in Teacher Education* 10 (Fall 1988): 35-39.

Reihman, Jacqueline M., Sara Varhus, and William R. Whipple. *Evaluating Honors Programs: An Outcomes Approach.* NCHC Monographs in Honors Education. Boise, ID: NCHC, 1990.

Reitano, Joanne. "Honors Programs and the Community College Mission." *National Honors Report* 17.4 (Winter 1997): 24-27.

Rhode, Robert T. "The Disenchanted Generation." *National Honors Report* 13.3 (Fall 1993): 20-22.

—. "Preparing the Under-Prepared." *National Honors Report* 13.4 (Winter 1993): 21-24.

—. "Welcome to Honors Teaching." *National Honors Report* 14.2 (Summer 1993): 11-14.

—. "What Should Every Honors Student Know?" *National Honors Report* 10.3 (Fall 1989): 8-9.

Rich, Stanley. "Motivating Students through Honors Contracts." *National Honors Report* 18.2 (Summer 1997): 17-19.

Riek, Ellen. "Building Community and Fostering Excellence through the Writing Process." *HIP* 1 (2005): 103-108.

Rinn, Anne N. "Academic and Social Effects of Living in Honors Residence Halls." *JNCHC* 5.2 (2004): 67-79.

—. "Rhodes Scholarships, Frank Aydelotte, and Collegiate Honors Education." *JNCHC* 4.1 (2003): 27-39.

Ritchey, Nate. "Baptism into Honors." *National Honors Report* 16.3 (Fall 1995): 24-27.

Roberts, Leslie. "Eco-Urban Year Honors Program." *Visions: The Journal of Applied Research for the Florida Association of Community Colleges* 2.2 (Summer 1999): 55-6.

Robertson, Julie Fisher, and Donna Rane-Szostak. "Helping Honors Students Improve Critical Thinking." *JNCHC* 2.1 (2001): 41-52.

Rochelson, Meri-Jane. "Florida International University." *JNCHC* 3.2 (2002): 48.

Roemer, Robert E. "The *Forum for Honors*: An Expanded View." *JNCHC* 5.1 (2004): 29-32.

Rutan, Elizabeth, and Kyle Johnson. "The Perceptions of Honors Students: A Case Study." *National Honors Report* 16.1 (Spring 1995): 27-28.

Sanders, Sara L., and Janet S. Files. "Seeing the World Anew: Creative Arts in the Honors Curriculum." *JNCHC* 2.2 (2001): 47-57.

Savage, Hallie E. Rev. of *How to Write a BA Thesis: A Practical Guide from Your First Ideas to Your Finished Paper*, by Charles Lipson." *JNCHC* 6.2 (2005): 139-40.

Schlenker, Jon A. "Technology, Distance Education, and Honors." *JNCHC* 3.2 (2002): 17-22.

Schneider, Carol. "Presidents' Campaign for the Advancement of Liberal Learning (CALL)." *JNCHC* 3.1 (2002): 33-35.

Schuman, Samuel. "Acadia or Arcadia: Reflections on the Maine Coast Semester Honors Program." *Forum for Honors* 20.3 (Winter/Spring 1991): 9-13.

—. *Beginning in Honors: A Handbook.* 3rd Edition. NCHC, 1995.

—. *Beginning in Honors: A Handbook.* 4th Edition. Lincoln: National Collegiate Honors Council, 2006.

—. "Catherine's Plenty." *JNCHC* 1.1 (2000): 7-8.

—. "Cultivating: Some Thoughts on the NCHC's Future." *JNCHC* 2.1 (2001): 69-72.

—. *Honors Programs at Smaller Colleges.* Boise, ID: National Collegiate Honors Council, 1988.

—. "Honors Scholarship and Forum for Honors." *JNCHC* 5.1 (2004): 19-23.

—. "Labors of Love." *JNCHC* 1.1 (2000): 85-90.

—. "Teaching Honors." *JNCHC* 6.2 (2005): 31-33.

—. "We THINK We Can, We THINK We Can...." *JNCHC* 3.1 (2002): 15-18.

Sederberg, Peter C. "Characteristics of the Contemporary Honors College: A Descriptive Analysis of a Survey of NCHC Member Colleges." *JNCHC* 6.2 (2005): 121-36.

—. "Simple, Pure, and True: An Emergent Vision of Liberal Learning at the Research University." *JNCHC* 5.1 (2004): 43-51.

Sedlack, R. Guy. "The Student Grants Program: Seeking a Different Approach to the Capable Student." *National Honors Report* 7.2 (Summer 1986): 1+.

—. "Honors and the Electronic Age." *National Honors Report* 17.2 (Summer 1996): 38-36.

—. "The Honors Evaluation Committee Report on The Basic Characteristics of a Fully-Developed Honors Program: Research Toward Creating a Dialogue." *National Honors Report* 18.1 (Spring 1997): 31-41.

Senior, William A. "College and University Honors Programs: A Select Bibliography." *National Honors Report* 20.4 (Winter 2000): 16-22.

Sheperd, Gordon, and Gary Sheperd. "War Attitudes and Ideological Orientations of Honors Directors in American Higher Education." *Journal of Higher Education* 67.3 (May/Jun 1996): 298-321.

Shepherd, Ursula L. "Creative Approaches to Teaching Science in an Honors Setting." *JNCHC* 1.2 (2000): 53-61.

Skau, G. "Honors Programs at the Community College." 1989. ERIC ED307938.

Skewes, Juan Carlos, Carlos Alberto Cioce Sampaio, and Frederick J. Conway. "Honors in Chile: New Engagements in the Higher Education System." *HIP* 2 (2006): 15-26.

Smith, Matthew L., and Jason C. Vallee. "Leadership in Scholarship Program." *HIP* 2 (2006): 43-48.

Sodt, James D. "Reflections from the Edge: Change, Reengineering, and Honors." *National Honors Report* 18.1 (Spring 1997): 45-49.

Sorensen, Jean. "Documenting the Achievements of Our Students without Compromising Excellence." *JNCHC* 7.1 (2006): 33-36.

Spurrier, Bob. "Technology and the NCHC." *JNCHC* 3.2 (2002): 11-15.

Spurrier, Robert. "Ten Suggestions for Using Your Institutional Accreditation Process to Benefit Your Honors Program." *National Honors Report* 16.2 (Summer 1995): 21-25.

Spurrier, Robert, and Natalie Bruner. "Developing a Parallel Honors Advising System." *National Honors Report* 15.1 (Spring 1994): 5-8.

Stanlick, Nancy A. "Creating an Honors Community: A Virtue Ethics Approach." *JNCHC* 7.1 (2006): 75-92.

Stephens, Jane, and J.A. Eison. "A Comparative Investigation of Honors and Non-Honors Students." *Forum For Honors* (Fall/Winter 1986/7): 17-25.

Stocker, Marilyn J. "'No Turning Back': The Honors Semester as Catalyst for Developmental Change." *Forum for Honors* 20.3 (Winter/Spring 1991): 51-66.

Stoller, Richard. "Honors Selection Processes: A Typology and Some Reflections." *JNCHC* 5.1 (2004): 79-85.

Stowell, Jeffrey R. "Using Peer Review in Honors Courses." *HIP* 2 (2006): 97-100.

Strong, Paul. "Honors as Skunkworks." *JNCHC* 7.1 (2006): 53-55.

—. "Serious Play." *JNCHC* 1.1 (2000): 91-97.

Stuckey, Mary E., and Elizabeth L. Macy. "Best at Not Being Good Enough." *National Honors Report* 16.1 (Spring 1995): 29-32.

Sulik, Robert P. "An Honors College Advanced Freshman Studies Program." *National Honors Report* 15.1 (Spring 1994): 9-11.

Sullivan, Robert R., and Karin R. Randolph. *Ivy League Programs at State School Prices.* New York: Prentice Hall, 1994.

Swafford, James. "Jump-Starting Honors Community with Introductory Biographies." *HIP* 1 (2005): 123-127.

Swanson, Joseph. "Toward Community: The Relationship between Religiosity and Silence in the Works of Søren Kierkegaard." *JNCHC* 4.2 (2003): 11-18.

Szumowski, Margaret C. "Honors Students in the Creative Writing Classroom: Sequence and Community." *JNCHC* 2.2 (2001): 59-70.

Teaching and Learning in Honors. Ed. Cheryl L. Fuiks and Larry Clark. National Collegiate Honors Council, 2000.

Tebbs, Trevor J. "University of Connecticut." *JNCHC* 3.2 (2002): 47.

Tenhet, Nancy, Juanita Flanders, Jeanne Wells Cook, and Margaret Jane Stauble. "Collaborative Teaching of English and Information Literacy in the Community College Honors Program." *JNCHC* 3.2 (2002): 29-32.

Terrill, Marty. "Tailoring an Honors Program to Your Institution." 1991. ERIC ED333953.

Tighe, Mary Ann. "Literacy, Society, and the Individual: An Honors Course Integrating Knowledge and Experience." *National Honors Report* 14. 2 (Summer 1993): 19-21.

Todd, Susan M. "Scholars and Strategies: Honors Programs in Community Colleges." *Community College Review* 16 (Summer 1988): 18-29.

Tomlinson, Susan. "The Curiosity Shop (Or, How I Stopped Worrying About Delta Shapes and Started Teaching)." *JNCHC* 1.2 (2000): 33-51.

Triplet, Rodney. "The Honors Program."1998. ERIC ED316098.

Tucker, Don. "The Pickup Truck, Being a Scholarly Paper on the Efficiencies Effected by Modern Technology." *JNCHC* 3.2 (2002): 23-27.

Varadhan, Vasu. "The New World Information Order: Internationalizing the Honors Curriculum." *National Honors Report* 13.4 (Winter 1993): 33-34.

Varhus, Sara. "Empathy and the Questioning Spirit in Liberal Education: Reports from the Field." *JNCHC* 1.1 (2000): 32-40.

Viau, Elizabeth Anne. "Using the Honors Discussion Format with Non-Honors Students." *National Honors Report* 15.2 (Summer 1994): 17-19.

Von Blum, Paul. "Curating Art Exhibitions: Promoting Active Honors Education." *National Honors Report* 18.3 (Fall 1997): 30-33.

Vowell, Faye N., et al. "Midwifing an Honors Culture." *National Honors Report* 15.1 (Spring 1994): 17-19.

Wade, Beverly D, and Calvin Walker. "Assessing the Effect of Various Academic Parameters on the Academic Performance of Honors Students at Southern University-BR." *Education* 115 (Fall 1994): 63-69.

Wainscott, Steve. "It's Ten O'Clock: Do You Know Where Your Students Are?" *JNCHC* 2.1 (2001): 87-89.

Wall, John. "North Carolina State University." *JNCHC* 3.2 (2002): 53.

Walshe, Emily. "Athena, Telemachus, and the Honors Student Odyssey: The Academic Librarian as an Agent in Mentored Learning." *JNCHC* 6.1 (2005): 85-93.

Walter-Fromson, Ann E., Paul L. Leslie, and Richard A. Rowe. "When Students Take the Lead: Evaluation of a Student-Directed Seminar." *Forum for Honors* 21.2 Summer/Fall 1992): 3-9.

Wang, Alvin, Crystal Espinosa, Cassandra Long, and Anik Patel. "Team Leaders and the Honors Freshman-Year Experience." *HIP* 1 (2005): 129-138.

Ward, Kelly. "Service Learning in Honors Education: Involving Students in Citizenship and Social Change." *National Honors Report* 16.3 (Fall 1995): 45-46.

Watkins, Beverly T. "Experimental Honors Seminar in Physics Explores Uses of Computers in Classroom." *Chronicle of Higher Education* 38.2 (Sept. 4 1991): A29.

Werth, Alexander. "On the Benefits of Teaching Honors." *HIP* 1 (2005): 43-48.

—. "Unity in Diversity: The Virtues of a Metadisciplinary Perspective in Liberal Arts Education." *JNCHC* 4.2 (2003): 35-51.

West, Betsy. "An Architect's Foray into Honors." *JNCHC* 2.2 (2001): 15-20.

West, Rinda. "Disney Defrocked: A Field Study of Coyotes by an Honors Environmental Science Class." *National Honors Report* 16.2 (Summer 1995): 42-46.

—. "Teaching and Learning." *National Honors Report* 12.4 (Winter 1997): 33-34.

West, Rinda, et al. "The Liberal Art of Science: Science and History in an Honors Program." Des Plaines, IL: Oakton Community College, 1991. ERIC ED351048.

Willerton, Chris, et al. "Corporate Cultures within Institutions." *National Honors Report* 16.4 (Winter 1996): 16-24.

Wilson, Anne M., and Melissa Ludwa. "They Filched Our Program! How to Turn That into a Good Thing." *HIP* 2 (2006): 73-83.

Wilson, John. "Loaded Canons: The Battle for Culture in the University." *Forum for Honors* 21.1 (Winter/Spring 1992): 12-17.

Wilson, Robin. "A Community College Propels Graduates to Top Universities." *The Chronicle of Higher Education* 39 (Sept. 9 1992): A33-4.

Wilson, Steffen. "Using Learning Outcomes Assessment in Honors as a Defense Against Proposed Standardized Testing." *JNCHC* 7.1 (2006): 27-31.

Wilson, Steffen Pope, and Rose M. Perrine. "We Know They are Smart, but Have They Learned Anything?: Strategies for Assessing Learning in Honors." *HIP* 1 (2005): 27-37.

Winter, Richard. "Education or Grading? Arguments for a Non-Subdivided Honours Degree." *Studies in Higher Education* 18.3 (1993): 363-77.

Witte, Alison, and Philip Taylor. "Glenville State College Presidential Scholars Program." *JNCHC* 3.2 (2002): 49.

Witthuhn, Burton, et al. "A Strategy for Honor Students for Timely Baccalaureate Degree Search." *National Honors Report* 17.3 (Fall 1996): 38-40.

Wittig, A.F., et al. "Gender, Personality Characteristics and Academic Preparation as Factors for Achievement and Attrition of Honors Students." *Forum for Honors* 17.1-2 (1986-7): 26-35.

Wolfensberger, Marca V. C. "Qualities Honours Students Look for in Faculty and Courses." *JNCHC* 5.2 (2004): 55-66.

Wolfensberger, Marca V. C., Pierre J. van Eijl, and Albert Pilot. "Honours Programmes as Laboratories of Innovation: A Perspective from the Netherlands." *JNCHC* 5.1 (2004): 115-41.

Workinger, William. "Setting up an Honors Program." *Music Educators Journal* 79.8 (April 1993): 29-32.

Worrall, Patricia B. "'Expressive Technology': Multimedia Projects in Honors Courses." *JNCHC* 2.2 (2001): 83-91.

Yarrison, Betsy Greenleaf. "Honors for Grown-Ups: Educations for Non-Traditional Students." *National Honors Report* 18.3 (Fall 1997): 20-28.

Younger, Kelly. "Honors, Inc." *JNCHC* 5.1 (2004): 63-77.

Zane, Len. "Honors as an Adjective: Response to Jay Freyman." *JNCHC* 6.2 (2005): 35-37.

—. "The Honors Gap." *National Honors Report* 13.4 (Winter 1993): 24-25.

—. "A Physicist in Honors." *JNCHC* 1.2 (2000): 13-20.

—. "A Small Step." *JNCHC* 2.1 (2001): 77-81.

Notes

Notes

The official guide to NCHC member institutions has a new name, a new look, and expanded information!

- Peter Sederberg's essay on honors colleges brings readers up to date on how they differ from honors programs.
- Lydia Lyons' new essay shows how two-year honors experiences can benefit students and lead them to great choices in completing the bachelor's degree and going beyond.
- Kate Bruce adds an enriched view of travels with honors students.

These and all the other helpful essays on scholarships, community, Honors Semesters, parenting, and partnerships make the 4th edition a must in your collection of current honors reference works. *This book is STILL the only honors guide on the market*, and it is your best tool for networking with local high schools and community colleges as well as for keeping your administration up to date on what your program offers.

Peterson's Smart Choices retails for $29.95.
**NCHC members may order copies for only $20 each
(a 33% savings) and get free shipping!**
Send check or money order payable to NCHC to:
NCHC, 1100 NRC-UNL, 540 N. 16th St., Lincoln, NE 68588-0627.
Or call (402) 472-9150 to order with a credit card.

NCHC PUBLICATION ORDER FORM

Purchases may be made by calling (402) 472-9150, emailing nchc@unlserv.unl.edu, or mailing a check or money order payable to NCHC to:

NCHC • 1100 Neihardt Residence Center • University of Nebraska-Lincoln
540 N. 16th Street • Lincoln, NE 68588-0627

FEIN 52–1188042

	Member	Non-Member	No. of Copies	Amount This Item
Monographs:				
Assessing and Evaluating Honors Programs and Honors Colleges: A Practical Handbook	$10.00	$12.50		
Beginning in Honors: A Handbook (4th Ed.)	$10.00	$12.50		
A Handbook for Honors Administrators	$10.00	$12.50		
A Handbook for Honors Programs at Two-Year Colleges	$10.00	$12.50		
Honors Composition: Historical Perspectives and Contemporary Practices	$10.00	$12.50		
Honors Programs at Smaller Colleges (2nd Ed.)	$10.00	$12.50		
Innovations in Undergraduate Research and Honors Education: Proceedings of the Second Schreyer National Conference	$10.00	$12.50		
Place as Text: Approaches to Active Learning	$10.00	$12.50		
Teaching and Learning in Honors	$10.00	$12.50		
Journals:				
Journal of the National Collegiate Honors Council (JNCHC) Specify Volume/Issue ____/____	$10.00	$12.50		
Honors in Practice (HIP) Specify Volume _____	$10.00	$12.50		
Other Publications:				
Peterson's Smart Choices (The official NCHC guide to Honors Programs & Colleges)	$20.00	$29.95		
NCHC Handbook	$15.00	$20.00		
Total Copies Ordered and Total Amount Paid: _____ $_____				

Apply a 20% discount if 10+ copies are purchased.

Name _____

Institution _____

Address _____

City, State, Zip _____

Phone _____ Fax _____ Email _____

NATIONAL COLLEGIATE HONORS COUNCIL
MONOGRAPHS & JOURNALS

Assessing and Evaluating Honors Programs and Honors Colleges: A Practical Handbook by Rosalie Otero and Robert Spurrier (2005, 98pp). This monograph includes an overview of assessment and evaluation practices and strategies. It explores the process for conducting self-studies and discusses the differences between using consultants and external reviewers. It provides a guide to conducting external reviews along with information about how to become an NCHC-recommended Site Visitor. A dozen appendices provide examples of "best practices."

Beginning in Honors: A Handbook by Samuel Schuman (Fourth Edition, 2006, 80pp). Advice on starting a new honors program. Covers budgets, recruiting students and faculty, physical plant, administrative concerns, curriculum design, and descriptions of some model programs.

A Handbook for Honors Administrators by Ada Long (1995, 117pp). Everything an honors administrator needs to know including a description of some models of Honors Administration.

A Handbook for Honors Programs at Two-Year Colleges by Theresa James (2006, 136pp). A useful handbook for two-year schools contemplating beginning or redesigning their honors program and for four-year schools doing likewise or wanting to increase awareness about two-year programs and articulation agreements. Contains extensive appendices about honors contracts and a comprehensive bibliography on honors education.

Honors Composition: Historical Perspectives and Contemporary Practices by Annmarie Guzy (2003 182 pp). Parallel historical developments in honors and composition studies; contemporary honors writing projects ranging from admission essays to theses as reported by over 300 NCHC members.

Honors Programs at Smaller Colleges by Samuel Schuman (Second Edition, 1999, 53pp). How to implement an honors program, with particular emphasis on colleges with fewer than 3000 students.

Innovations in Undergraduate Research and Honors Education: Proceedings of the Second Schreyer National Conference Edited by Josephine M. Carubia and Renata S. Engel (2004 145pp). Essays on the importance of undergraduate research, course models, connections to service learning, and learning strategies that support undergraduate research.

Place as Text: Approaches to Active Learning edited by Bernice Braid and Ada Long (2000, 104pp). Information and practical advice on the experiential pedagogies developed within NCHC during the past 25 years, using Honors Semesters and City as Text© as models, along with suggestions for how to adapt these models to a variety of educational contexts.

Teaching and Learning in Honors edited by Cheryl L. Fuiks and Larry Clark (2000, 128 pp). Presents a variety of perspectives on teaching and learning useful to anyone developing new or renovating established honors curricula.

Journal of the National Collegiate Honors Council (*JNCHC*) is a semi-annual periodical featuring scholarly articles on honors education. Articles may include analyses of trends in teaching methodology, articles on interdisciplinary efforts, discussions of problems common to honors programs, items on the national higher education agenda, and presentations of emergent issues relevant to honors education.

Honors in Practice (*HIP*) is an annual journal that accomodates the need and desire for articles about nuts and bolts practices by featuring practical and descriptive essays on topics such as successful honors courses, suggestions for out-of-class experiences, administrative issues, and other topics of interest to honors administrators, faculty and students.

NCHC Handbook. Included are lists of all NCHC members, NCHC Constitution and Bylaws, committees and committee charges, and other useful information.